Listening to the Body

Delta Books of Interest

THE CLOUD OF UNKNOWING
Introductory commentary and translation by Ira Progoff

EMERGENCE: The Rebirth of the Sacred
David Spangler

EMPOWERMENT: The Art of Creating Your Life
as You Want It
David Gershon and Gail Straub

THE MASTER GAME
Robert S. de Ropp

MIND AS HEALER, MIND AS SLAYER
Kenneth R. Pelletier

ROLLING THUNDER
Doug Boyd

THE SUPREME ADVENTURE
Peter Hayes

Robert Masters & Jean Houston

LISTENING TO THE BODY

The Psychophysical Way to Health and Awareness

Illustrations by Doris Rodewig

A DELTA BOOK
Published by
Dell Publishing
a division of
Bantam Doubleday Dell Publishing Group, Inc.
666 Fifth Avenue
New York, New York 10103

ISBN: 0-385-28577-9

Printed in the United States of America

Published simultaneously in Canada

One previous Delta edition

New Delta edition—November 1989

10 9 8 7 6 5 4 3 2 1

VB

Dedicated to our friend
DR. MOSHE FELDENKRAIS,
blazer of trails in
the jungle of the brain

Contents

Foreword

TO THE READER of this important and highly original book, reeducation may be taken as a simple, self-understood matter. The clear writing, the gradual passage from easy to more complex exercises may lull the reader into complacent agreement.

On second reading, however, one would appreciate the erudition, the width of the approach, and the originality of the content.

Reeducation is frequently understood as going over the original education to improve it. But the authors present something much more important than that. They guide the reader to educate himself in matters and ways that were almost certainly never included in the original education.

In fact, they take the reader a step ahead of where he or she left his or her education—the psychophysical one, of course, not the academic one. The step is not a continuation of what one has experienced before, but a new kind of self-education. It is a kind that will bring the reader to further his or her own growth as a person from where the growth was left to take its own course in the roughness and inconsistency of the hazards of life.

For many, this book will be *real* education at last. The book is, therefore, much more than its title suggests.

I believe that this sort of education leads to a new period of personality growth with versatility ramifications. I wish the reader the success that can result from this venture.

MOSHE FELDENKRAIS
49 Nachmani St.
Tel-Aviv

Introduction

EDUCATION SHOULD, but does not, teach us to make effective use of our bodies and our minds. We are not taught the interrelatedness of movement, sensing, thinking, and feeling functions, or how mind and body interact to determine what we are and what we can do. We are not even taught how to use our bodies efficiently so as to avoid damage to the organism. Nor are we given any inkling of the true range of our human potentials, much less how to use them productively. By suppressing many of our potentials, we develop the personality (and doubtless the brain also) in an imbalanced way. Adequate awareness of the body and of body-mind interactions is basic self-knowledge, and until these defects are remedied, education will always fail—fundamentally. Whatever *is* learned and taught by individuals who are thus handicapped by basic self-ignorance cannot be learned or taught as well as it might be. We will demonstrate to you repeatedly the accuracy and importance of the statements just made. However, we would not do that unless we could also offer remedies.

We will illustrate briefly: Please read just to the end of this paragraph, no further. When you have completed the paragraph, please go back and read the first paragraph again. Please read it with *concentration,* trying to be certain that you read every word, and that you really understand what is being said. Please do that *now,* and when you have done it, read on.

If you have made the experiment, try to remember what happened when you tried to concentrate. If you are like most people, your muscles tensed and your breathing was disrupted. Read *this* paragraph once again, with *concentration,* and observe what you do.

Those readers who are able to observe themselves closely are likely to have recognized the tension and the interference with breathing as they reread the last paragraph. If you are sitting as you read, it is likely that you drew your shoulders closer together, just a little. Probably there were other changes. It is common to frown or tense the facial muscles, and often the eyes become less mobile. These changes in the muscles, posture, and breathing are typically unconscious. But they are important for many reasons, not the least of which is that these unconscious tensions thwart the original purpose, competing with and undermining the effort to concentrate. Perhaps worse, such habitual patterns of bad body use erode both the body and the mind. They demonstrate clearly the need for a greater self-awareness, since it is only through increased awareness that they can be eliminated.

This book is intended to be read, but even more to be applied. It details a number of exercises—*experiences* might be a better description—which you can do and, by doing, come to know yourself better, understand yourself better, and especially *use* yourself better, thus improving your health and effectiveness in many ways.

Since a method requires a name, we will speak of *Psychophysical Reeducation. Psychophysical,* since we will avoid any false separation of the mental from the physical, a separation which does not exist in any human action. *Reeducation,* since the work consists first of unlearning the inappropriate ways of using ourselves to which we have become conditioned, then of rediscovering what we once possessed, or would have possessed had we developed without mishap. The method not only makes available to us capacities hitherto only latent, it also develops the capacities we have beyond their present limits.

The exercises in this book were created by one of the authors (R.M.) and have been taught and modified by both of us. One of the authors (J.H.) has worked mainly with groups, introducing the method to thousands of persons throughout the United States and also in Canada and Europe. The other author has worked more intensively with individuals, including training some teachers. Both of us have had ample occasion to observe the effects which we describe.

The exercises make extensive use of a unique teaching method devised by Moshe Feldenkrais, to whom the book is dedicated. More of his insights and findings have been used than it is practical to credit to him. However, responsibility for the exercises and statements made rests, of course, with the authors, who have drawn on their many years of research in order to extend the psychophysical approach in directions not previously taken.

Our experimental studies of consciousness, human potentials, the creative process, sensory imageries, psychodynamics, and various other aspects of human experience and functioning have naturally influenced our understandings, our ways of approaching problems, and the writing of this book. Thus, for example, we utilize more psychological techniques within the psychophysical context than others have done. By so doing we hope to act more directly on some thinking and feeling functions and to make different uses of the brain and nervous system.

The scope of application of psychophysical methods appears to be so vast that virtually any mind-body process can be worked with and improved. In fact, a main premise underlying this book is that man is almost infinitely malleable—the particular individual as well as mankind in general. Moreover, voluntary conscious control of many processes and functions that are seemingly involuntary may well be possible. It is only a question of finding the appropriate means, since few limits can be found to the nervous system's capacity to modify the mind-body, not at all excluding the system itself. There is evidence for this already in the recognized diversities of the billions of people who have lived on this earth. In general, whatever potential is manifested by even one individual is part of the *human* potential, realizable by many.

The work you will undertake here will not lead you to the outer limits of your potential for change, whatever those might be. Moving toward such unknowns is a project for explorers with very special skills. We take you, rather, over mapped terrain, where experiences are predictable and, as we have seen again and again, both exciting and productive.

No exercises or sports you might undertake are safer or less likely to lead to even minimal strain than are the exercises presented in this book. If that proves not to be so, then you have done them in ways other than those clearly specified. Whenever even one exercise is done, you will experience some kind of improvement. Moreover, the effects are cumulative, so that over a period of time some major beneficial changes will occur—changes more far-reaching and comprehensive than any attainable when just body or just mind is worked with, as in almost all present modes of education.

We invite you to participate in *experiences* which are both revelations and adventures in progressive self-discovery. They are potent and, given the chance, will enrich your life in ways both hoped for and undreamed of.

Acknowledgments

MANY INDIVIDUALS have contributed to the work and understandings set forth in this book.

The major contribution of Moshe Feldenkrais has already been mentioned in both the dedication and the introduction.

Dr. Wilfred Barlow and Marjory Barlow of the Alexander Institute in London spent many weeks demonstrating to us Alexander's psychophysical methods and discussing as well their own work, including the training of teachers.

We spent some years in the practice of yoga and studied in particular with Swami Karmananda.

Dr. Margaret Mead has made many helpful observations and has had some illuminating things to say about movement, posture, and "use" in different cultures.

With Pak Subur, master teacher of the Indonesian martial art of Pentjak-Silat, we have had helpful discussions about mind-body interactions from both Eastern and Western perspectives.

Kung-fu black belt Michele Carrier has also been helpful in comparing martial arts understandings with our own.

Lillemor Johnsen of Norway introduced us to her own unique contributions to psychophysical methods, especially as applied to psychotherapy.

Kolman Korentayer, devoted, indefatigable assistant to Moshe Feldenkrais, has aided our investigations in a good many significant ways.

Ron Bernstein, our literary agent, is an author's dream come true.

Ilana Rubenfeld, who has developed her own Gestalt–Alexander–Feldenkrais synthesis, made suggestions concerning the manuscript.

Micaela Kelly has been helpful in more ways than we can mention.

Over the years we have worked with uncounted thousands of research subjects, patients, and students, who have thus enabled us to learn at firsthand much that now informs this book.

Finally, our Old English mastiff, Titan, obliged us to learn, in order to help him, a good deal about muscles and bones the veterinarians seem not to know, and which sheds some light on human problems also.

Part *1*

Psychophysical Reeducation

The Psychophysical Approach

EVERYONE KNOWS that mind and body interact, the one affecting the other. Sexual fantasies and dreams, for example, trigger complicated bodily changes. Drugs act upon the mind through the body, releasing emotions, ideas, and images. When Ebenezer Scrooge's everyday world began to get stranger and stranger, he surmised that some undigested morsel of meat might be the cause, although happily for him the cause was not so mundane. Even as children we learn, or somehow know, that we can alter our mental states by rocking, whirling, and by other means. Many children also know that physical pain can be banished by intense involvement in either mental or physical activity.

As people go through life they acquire either random or specialized knowledge of mind-body interactions which they can apply in a variety of ways. Some learn to relax by "thinking pleasant thoughts," and some learn to heal themselves of various ailments by "thinking good thoughts." Others run, swim, or walk as much for the mental and emotional benefits as for any physical ones. In recent years, in Western countries, millions of people have found that some form of meditation can improve them physically as well as mentally. A smaller number, working with biofeedback, have learned that they can control even some "involuntary" processes, such as blood flow, skin temperature, heart rate, and brain waves. In biofeedback, mind, body, and machine work together to effect what may be thought of as bodily changes, such as altered blood flow to banish a headache, or what may be thought of as mainly mental changes, as when brain waves are controlled to produce states of tranquility or creative reverie. Almost all adults have experienced altered mental states produced by alcohol, tranquilizing drugs, coffee, nicotine, or other chemical substances which primarily affect the body. Mind-body interactions are a commonplace of everyday life for most people.

In the instances mentioned above, the physical or mental changes involved are generally produced intentionally and their causes are clearly recognized. Thus, the effect of mind on body or body on mind is readily observed. But apart from special cases of this sort, the body and the mind are in continuous interaction, affecting one another more or less profoundly and engendering changes of which the person is very often quite unaware. This is true to such an extent that the great majority of people do not have sufficient voluntary control of their bodies, their minds, or their behavior to prevent the serious unconscious injury they do themselves in many ways, both mental and physical. The normal condition of the human being as he goes about his activities more nearly resembles sleep than the alert waking state which he obviously thinks he is in. These, however, are statements which must be demonstrated to a person to be true, for one cannot understand them by an effort of the intellect alone, although he may give intellectual acquiescence. For real understanding, *experience* is required.

The same problem arises when we tell you, for example, that your experience of your body is more or less distorted, so that when you act according to your experience of your body, there will be a discrepancy between what you intend to do and think that you do on the one hand, and what you actually do—without knowing that you do it—on the other. Similarly, if we tell you that much that you do is entirely unconscious, how can you really understand what is meant unless you are able to make conscious what was unconscious?

In the case of this book, we thus arrive at something curious: The person who can understand it merely by reading it probably is wasting his time. If he *cannot* understand it just by reading it, however, that plainly demonstrates his urgent need for the experiences which alone can enable him to understand. When he has achieved this, *then* he will know that what obstructed him before had nothing much to do with his intellect or the extent of his academic learning. He will realize that the obstruction was a gap in self-knowledge, a lack of sufficient awareness of his own body-mind: sensing, feeling, thinking, brain and nervous system, muscles and bones, mind and body apprehended as aspects of an interdependent, interactive whole.

Since you will change if you apply this book's method, it is our obligation to demonstrate clearly and experientially what the changes will be as well as how to make them. Our approach is to show you what the situation is with yourself, the ways in which it can be improved, and how to go about it if you decide you want to do so. After that, you will proceed by your own efforts.

As you read, we ask you to refrain from using only mental processes to accept or reject what is said. Since this is a book about a psychophysical approach, it provides you with many opportunities to let both your body and your mind, or body-mind, participate to an extraordinary degree in your experiencing. On the basis of *experience,* accept or reject. Our promise is that through your experience you will reach an understanding which must otherwise elude you.

Psychophysical Reeducation

Psychophysical Reeducation exercises work with body and mind together to improve specific and overall functioning and to bring you closer to your potential. A great many diverse, gentle movements are evoked, always with attention being drawn to the movements and the accompanying sensations. As you learn, with a minimum of effort, to pay attention to your body, you will find that your body will become more accessible to your mind, and as this happens, it will function better. You will learn that the body can function optimally only when "minded," or when there is awareness, and you will discover the extent to which awareness was previously lacking.

Some exercises do not work with movements of the muscles and bones, but with "movements" of attention, shifting its focus to bring about various changes in the body. Or "movements" are made in the imagination only, after which you will discover that these have enabled the body to move better, sometimes with more improvement than physical movements could have achieved. In all cases, there is a simultaneous working with body and mind, or body-mind, to achieve the aimed-for results.

Not only are awareness and the ability to move and to sense enhanced; cognitive and feeling functions improve also, for the extensive changes in the brain's motor cortex which must precede changes in the muscular system affect adjacent brain areas as well: "Owing to the close proximity to the motor cortex of the brain structures dealing with thought and feeling, and the tendency of processes in the brain tissue to diffuse and spread to neighboring tissues, a drastic change in the motor cortex will have parallel effects on thinking and feeling."[1]

Psychophysical Reeducation is a neural reeducation,

[1] Moshe Feldenkrais, *Awareness Through Movement* (New York: Harper & Row, 1972), p. 39.

improving feedback from muscles and joints to the brain and reestablishing effective communication between the brain and parts of the body which have partially or altogether ceased to respond to voluntary control. As we progress, the surface of the body and the skeletal joints will come into awareness; posture will improve and the body, not so burdened by gravity, will feel much lighter; excessive efforts, which accompany almost all actions, will be eliminated or minimized. Hitherto unconscious patterns of muscular tensions will become conscious while, at the same time, the tensions will ease and the muscles will lengthen as we effectively alter patterns in the brain which served in the past to maintain the contractions. With these changes in the musculature, the body will become somewhat longer, the skeletal structure will assume a more natural alignment, with an improved condition of the skeletal joints productive of both better health and greater freedom of movement. But, again, we will not encounter changes in the body apart from corresponding mental, emotional, and other changes. It seems to be a general rule that an improved condition of the body fosters other improvements. Dissolution of muscular tension patterns, for example, is likely to mean reduced levels of anxiety. Some habits will lose much of their force, so that breaking free of them will be much easier. Similarly, some blocks and inhibitions will be weakened or simply vanish. We have seen these results often, and such changes invariably have been constructive ones. Nothing that was valued has ever been lost. It is what impairs or destroys the body that is likely to be destructive to us in other ways.

The End-gaining Syndrome

An almost universal pattern of behavior which the exercises will go far to eliminate was called *end-gaining* by F. Matthias Alexander, brilliant pioneer of psychophysical methods. End-gaining behavior is the habit of focusing so intensely on the goal, or end, to be gained that the means employed to gain it are ignored. Those means, then, cannot be efficient, and they are very often harmful. We all resemble, to some extent, the child whose ball rolls into the street and who is so intent on recovering the ball that he goes dashing out into the street without giving any thought to the traffic and is run down by an automobile. End-gaining behavior produces unconscious, or minimally conscious, action, so that the fact that it is harmful is not registered. Were it not for sensory impairment, from which almost all of us suffer, then at least we would not persist in actions which otherwise would be sensed as painful. The following example illustrates:

If you ask a man to pick up a fairly heavy object, a chair, for instance, you will observe that he at once becomes fixated on his goal—the muscular effort he is going to make. Before he has even approached the chair, he will already have tensed the muscles he intends to use (arms, back, neck, etc.) and he will have done this according to his preconception of the effort needed. *The effort made will always be excessive.* As Alexander put it: "The kinesthetic system has not been taught to register correctly the tension or, in other words, to gauge accurately the amount of effort required to perform certain acts, *the expenditure of effort always being in excess of what is required* [our italics], an excellent instance of the lack of harmony in an untutored organism."[2] Moreover, the man's experience of the weight of the chair will be partly determined by his preconceptions and the magnitude of his effort, and only partly by the chair's actual weight. The chair will thus feel significantly lighter or heavier to one man than to another of approximately equal strength. It will feel lightest to the one who approaches lifting it without preconceptions and without any previous organization of his muscles, and who lifts by taking hold of the object and exerting only as much force as is required to overcome its resistance. If the kinesthetic system is extremely impaired and/or the muscles unusually contracted, then proportionately greater force will be used. One sees this in the case of certain neurotics whose efforts are so disproportionate to every task that the disparity is evident to all. In such a case, the state of the musculature, which is a component of the neurosis, is a more immediate cause of excessive effort than are any emotional factors.

There are other factors which determine the ease or difficulty of a task. One is the efficiency of the body's positioning and use—what Alexander called "assuming the position of greatest mechanical advantage." Another is social. If, for instance, a man is being observed, he may function quite differently than he would if no one else were present. He may be self-conscious, so that tension in the muscles increases and he becomes awk-

[2] F. M. Alexander, *Man's Supreme Inheritance* (London: Chaterson, 1946), pp. 58–9.

ward. Or, in another case, because he is being observed, he may perform the action better, though without conscious effort to do so.

More important than any individual case, however, as Alexander observed, almost all of us use excessive effort in practically everything we do. Thus what we have to consider is the waste of our energies over a lifetime, the effect of unnecessary tensions on our bodies over a lifetime, and the resultant damage which we do to our bodies and our lives—sometimes quickly, more often by slow erosion. Indeed, it is often possible to guess how difficult life is for an individual by noticing how much effort he squanders on actions which have little symbolic significance or affective content. By observing this end-gaining behavior as it manifests itself in trivial actions, one can imagine how this habit is applied to attaining all goals, great or small, and at what cost to the individual and to others around him.

Like most habits, the end-gaining syndrome is best dealt with not by a strenuous effort of the will and attempted suppression of all the manifestations of the habit, but rather by the acquisition of pleasurable ways of acting which allow us to relinquish the old ones without ever having to oppose them directly. Many of the psychophysical exercises are effective means of "letting go" of, rather than "overcoming," end-gaining behavior.

In doing the exercises there is never anything that you *have to* achieve. There is no competition and we ask you to avoid all strain and to do only what is easily within your means. We urge you to pay close attention to the sensations accompanying the various movements, but the novelty of the sensations will make this easier, since many of these movements have not been performed since childhood or infancy and are simply no longer familiar to you. Gradually, you will develop the habit of paying attention to the movements and sensations without any thought of a goal to be reached. Something, to be sure, will be achieved, but even after the exercise has become familiar, the results will often come as a surprise. In time you will develop a habit of attending without effort to the physical movements involved in all kinds of activities, not just when doing the exercises, but at all times. Then you will discover that more of your goals are reached, and reached more easily, without damage to yourself or others. These results are possible because, in addition to diverting some attention from the end to the means, the exercises correct or improve the body image.

Body and Body-as-experienced

The term *body image* as used here refers to the body as we *sense* it to be. Ideally it encompasses the entire surface of the body and the skeletal joints. In addition to our kinesthetic awareness of the body, the body image includes our appearance, how we see ourselves in the mirror or when we look at various parts of our body, and our notion about what we look like to others—which is sometimes quite different from how we really do look to others. The body image is an aspect of a larger, more comprehensive *self image,* which incorporates everything we believe ourselves to be.

It is easy to demonstrate—as you will see—that the body image does not necessarily coincide with the physical body, as ideally it should. Some parts are missing from everyone's body image, just as some are sensed very indistinctly and some are sensed in ways which distort the body's objective reality. Since we always act in accordance with our body image, it is important that the image approximate the objective body as nearly as possible. (Although this is true in general, there are special cases where a body image that excludes objective defects or limitations can allow an individual to function better than he might if the body image were factually correct.)

The body image acquires its gaps, its areas of vagueness, and its distortions in various ways. Pain, disuse and misuse of the body, and mental and emotional difficulties are among the factors which engender a disparity between the body and the body-as-experienced. Both the objective body and the body image are affected in countless ways by the larger self image, which also has its omissions and distortions.

Parts of the body and the interconnections between them fade from the image when they are not used. Sexual anxieties and other sex problems may cause the genitals to disappear from the body image, or to become faint—we may be unable to sense their presence without looking or touching. A schizophrenic may lose his bodily sensations just as completely as if the nerves were deadened. A man who has lost a limb may continue to sense the limb as present, the body image in this case retaining what the physical body has lost. Even those who think of themselves as paragons of health and good functioning are not likely to be able to sense clearly their middle toes or the backs of their heads, as compared to their lips or even their big and little toes.

In the case of the toes, the lack of clear sensing means that they are undifferentiated, incapable of separate movement. Such an incapacity is not natural, and it interferes with the flexibility of both foot and ankle, and perhaps other joints as well, so that walking is impeded. Many women have toes that overlap as a consequence of wearing narrow, pointed shoes, and serious health problems can eventually result. Going barefoot as much as possible makes for a healthier foot and better walking, and it can help to bring the foot and toes more clearly into the body image.

Similarly, wherever the body image has gaps, areas of vagueness, or distortions, functioning will be impeded to varying degrees and problems of a serious nature will sooner or later arise if we live long enough. Conversely, where there is a clear awareness, good functioning and health are likely to result. Adequate awareness of our bodies is also a major deterrent to accidental injury. When athletes and dancers are injured, it is frequently because there are gaps or distortions in the body image, so that they impose strains on themselves which they would not do if they sensed accurately what they were doing. The same can be said of many of the injuries so common among elderly people—falls, in particular—when they are not caused by dizziness or poor circulation. A greater awareness and a body image corresponding more closely to the objective body would prevent countless tragic accidents.

Psychophysical exercises bring into awareness those parts of the body which are not sensed or which are sensed only dimly. They also eliminate distortions from the body image. When we use our bodies more completely, we experience many more sensations and presumably make use of formerly unused or little-used neural pathways. The body comes back into the mind, so to speak, when we use it well, and particularly when we focus attention on the parts of the body we are using and the accompanying sensations, not only in those parts, but in other parts not obviously, but more subtly, involved. The kinesthetic sense is corrected as, by means of the movements, we repeatedly bring the various parts of the body to states much closer to optimal functioning. The sensations produced by good functioning are pleasurable, whereas those produced by poor functioning, if they are experienced at all, are displeasurable. The kinesthetic sense, and the nervous system generally, prefer such more pleasurable states and, with sufficient sensing of them, will make them the norm and will also protest departures from that norm, since these will be correctly experienced as displeasure.

Awareness

There is a useful distinction to be made between consciousness and awareness: "Awareness is consciousness together with a realization of what is happening within it or of what is going on within ourselves while we are conscious."[3] You are conscious of reading this book, but it is quite unlikely that you are aware of all the movements you are making from moment to moment as you read, or even of how your body is positioned. For example, do you know, without checking, whether the parts of your body are symmetrical or whether some parts twist one way and some another? Is your left shoulder higher or lower than the right, or are they level? What parts of your body move as you breathe? Many more questions might be asked. Your ability or inability to supply the answers would indicate the state of your awareness. Adequate awareness would mean that we know what we are doing when we act—when, for instance, we walk or stand still, sit down or get up. If we lack such awareness, we will certainly engage in many inefficient and harmful actions, as might be expected when we do not know what we are doing. Most of us not only do not know what we are doing, we don't even know that we don't know, such is the extent to which we have become strangers to ourselves.

The execution of an action by no means proves that we know, even superficially, what we are doing or how

[3] Feldenkrais, *Awareness Through Movement*, p. 50.

we do it. If we attempt to carry out an action with awareness—that is, to follow it in detail—we soon discover that even the simplest and most common of actions, such as getting up from a chair, is a mystery, and that we have no idea at all of how it is done. Do we contract the muscles of the stomach or of the back, do we tense the legs first, or tilt the body forward first, what do the eyes do, or the head? It is easy to demonstrate that man does not know what he is doing, right down to being unable to rise from a chair. He therefore has no choice but to return to his accustomed method, which is to give himself the order to get up and to leave it to the specialized organizations within himself to carry out the action as it pleases them, which means as he usually does.[4]

It is not just a matter of not paying attention; much that is involved in rising from a chair will escape us no matter how closely we attend to the action. So long as the body is deficient, so long as the kinesthetic sense is distorted, so long as we lack a cultivated awareness, we will not be able to know what we do in even this simple act. The problem was recognized long ago; the Buddha, for example, termed the awareness of which we speak "mindfulness." In view of what has been said, the reader may understand a little better than he would have otherwise the lesson of this discourse from the Buddhist *Satipatthana-sutta:*

"And how, O priests, does a priest live, as respects the body, observant of the body?

". . . O priests, a priest in walking thoroughly comprehends his walking, and in standing thoroughly com-

[4] Feldenkrais, *Awareness Through Movement*, p. 46.

prehends his standing, and in sitting thoroughly comprehends his sitting, and in lying down thoroughly comprehends his lying down, and in whatever state his body may be thoroughly comprehends that state.

"Thus he lives, either in his own person, as respects the body, observant of the body, or both in his own person and in other persons, as respects the body, observant of the body, either observant of origination in the body, or observant of destruction in the body, or observant of both origination and destruction in the body; and the recognition of the body by his intent contemplation is merely to the extent of this knowledge, merely to the extent of this contemplation, and he lives unattached, nor clings to anything in this world.

". . . But again, O priests, a priest, in advancing and retiring has an accurate comprehension of what he does; in looking and gazing has an accurate comprehension of what he does; in drawing in his arm and in stretching out his arm has an accurate comprehension of what he does; in wearing his cloak, his bowl, and his robes has an accurate comprehension of what he does; in eating, drinking, chewing, and tasting has an accurate comprehension of what he does; in easing his bowels and his bladder has an accurate comprehension of what he does; in walking, standing, sitting, sleeping, waking, talking, and being silent has an accurate comprehension of what he does."[5]

The priest (we might say the aware human being) is also told to be attentive to all his sensations, his emotions, his desires, the ways he is using his mind, his thoughts and perceptions, the totality of his experience at each and every moment. "Thus does a priest live . . ."

[5] Quoted in Jacob Needleman, *A Sense of the Cosmos* (New York: Doubleday 1975), pp. 152–3.

Such "mindfulness" not only assures the aware human being that he knows what he is doing, it also frees him from his subservience to his own unconscious processes. Only by ridding himself of compulsions from within can he hope to attain the Buddhist goal of nonattachment.

Perfect awareness is an ideal state which no one is likely to realize. However, a refined awareness which approximates the mindfulness of the Buddhist priest is by no means unattainable, nor does it require an "intent contemplation," if that implies an ongoing *effort*. In fact, if a continuous disciplined effort of the will and attention were required, it would place an all but insurmountable obstacle in the path of adequate awareness and good use of the body. Some spiritual disciplines do demand such rigors, so that their goals can only be reached by those who dedicate themselves completely to the work. But this means only that their methods are faulty, not that total dedication is the only way to reach the goal.

Difficult to believe as it may be for some, psychophysical exercises will, over a period of time, develop a degree of awareness which approximates that described in the ancient Buddhist text. *Such awareness becomes the person's natural state and is, for that reason, effortless.* The attention is drawn to the body by means of novel and pleasurable sensations stimulated by the great variety of movements, also performed without effort, or with minimal effort. *Awareness is cultivated as a habit,* formed as other habits are formed, without trying. Once attained, it is not readily lost, nor would anyone want to lose it. It is not obtrusive but subtle, and can be magnified by focusing the attention, for purposes of self-observation and self-correction or just for pleasure. Sufficient bodily awareness will also enhance the awareness of mental and emotional processes and so facilitate self-regulation. However, for a larger measure of control, specific work aimed at those processes also must be done.

The Buddhist text refers to awareness of both "origination and destruction" in the body. In our terms this means that the aware person may often be able to sense his needs and recognize difficulties almost as they originate. He can also become aware, for example, of the organization of the muscles affected by the brain as he thinks or imagines various actions. Such a refinement of awareness is usually achieved only after much work.

A developed awareness, as the text suggests, extends to an increased awareness of others, and of the world in general. The aware individual not only senses more, and more truly, but functions more effectively, with less clumsiness, mental as well as physical. He will avoid, or minimize, "stupid" mistakes—for what is called "stupidity" is very often a shortcoming of awareness, not of intellect.

The Use of the Self

THE PARTS AND FUNCTIONS of the self are more intricately linked in the human mind-body system than we would ever guess from our own untutored self-awareness. No one has as yet even come close to understanding the full complexity and the full capacities of the human being. Much remains to be learned about how we work, and our greatest achievements undoubtedly await the time when we attain that knowledge. Insofar as we can assess them, even the greatest of human beings have so far realized but a small fraction of the human potential. Genius has often been, in the words of Sartre, "a way out that one takes in particularly desperate circumstances"—an extreme over-development of a few capacities with an equally extreme underdevelopment of others.

How we function is determined by how we use our whole organism at any time and in any situation. If we use it only partially or misuse it, on the one hand, or if we use it more fully and efficiently, on the other, then we will accordingly fail or succeed in the larger sense— the degree to which we do manage to approach our own potential.

Many who have studied the matter have concluded that we use only five to ten percent of our physical and mental potential. It is urgent for our survival that we find ways to use more. There is also the matter of the quality of use, which applies, of course, only to potentials to which we have access. Our objectives must be both to use more of ourselves and to use ourselves better.

The notion of "use" was developed by Alexander, whose Principle states that *use affects functioning*. This may seem obvious, but when we grasp the full complexity of the concept of "use," we will begin to realize how profound this principle is. As we have already observed, there are many possible obstructions to good use of ourselves: our lack of awareness, the gaps in our body image, the distortions in our sensing. If we cannot use ourselves well, and if our use determines how we function, then our faulty use will necessarily mean that our functioning also will be faulty. If Alexander is correct, as we believe, then there is no way out of the difficulty but to achieve good use. Several examples will give a better understanding of how important use is.

In a far from atypical case, a young boy imitates his

father's posture—whether consciously or unconsciously matters little. He learns to stand with his shoulders drawn up and back, which in turn curves his spine, impairs his breathing, and inhibits the free movement of his pelvis, hip joints, and knees, thus impeding his walking and his running and hampering his functioning in various other ways as well. It may have taken the father several decades to arrive at such misuse of himself, but by emulation the son takes on the destructive pattern very quickly. He may retain some of this pattern throughout his lifetime, so that it comes to play a decisive part in shaping his personality, his thinking, his sensing, his responses to other people, and the responses he elicits from them. Along with his father's pattern of use, he may in time inherit his father's sexual problems, etc.

It is not unusual to find men who in many ways closely resemble their fathers, especially in their glaring defects. (In general, people imitate the defects of others much more readily than they imitate their strengths, as those who train actors know. Young actors who would learn from successful professionals almost always imitate the obvious mannerisms and other faults and miss the subtleties which have made their models so successful.)

The boy in our example will probably draw on many different sources, creating an eclectic use for himself, at least until his own use pattern is too rigid to allow any further imitation. In addition to acquiring uses by imitation, the boy makes original contributions. His mother shouts at him frequently, and he responds by cringing, hunching his already-misused shoulders and throwing his head a bit to the side, which produces a different kind of curve in his spine, displaces his rib cage, and tightens his pectoral muscles. In time, not only do these changes become permanent, but in various stress situations he responds with exaggerated versions of the original pattern. He also learns to hold his breath and to tense new muscles, which increases his anxiety and general inability to function in stress situations. Eventually, he will die of arteriosclerosis, bequeathed to him by his father and his mother, who loved him dearly and wanted "only the best" for him. On the other hand this individual, creative and intelligent, may have had a distinguished career, prospered financially far more than most, and so have died "a success" in the estimation of others. What he might have been had he managed, with help, to eliminate his patterns of misuse, we cannot know. But he surely would have been healthier and more autonomous, and he probably would have lived longer. Without so firm a muscular foundation, his neurosis might not have been so severe. In high school, he might have been the athlete he so much wanted to be but could not be because of his impaired movement and coordination and the poor breathing habits which caused him to tire easily. Then his failure at sports would not have damaged his self-image and, because of that, his social relationships. He might have made a successful marriage instead of several unsuccessful ones. The chronic tensions and habitual overreactions to emotional stress would not have caused his premature death. This barely scratches the surface of the principle of use and the ways it affected the life of this individual.

His use might have been corrected at any time and his life set upon a different course. However, his misuse was never recognized, much less corrected. His health was generally considered normal, although later he was considered to have serious emotional problems. Until his arteriosclerosis was far advanced, his life might have been prolonged and his health greatly improved by a correction of his use. The emotional effects of various difficulties which had occurred in his life could not, of course, be erased, but a breaking up of the habitual mind-body responses and behavior patterns might have allowed him to form new and successful relationships, thus minimizing the impact of his past failures.

Dr. Wilfred Barlow, medical director of the Alexander Institute in London, briefly summarizes the actual case history of a man whose life is almost irretrievably ruined by long-standing misuse:

Dr. James P, a chest physician, has been worried for some time by increasing depression and a constant pain in his neck. He assuages it with liberal doses of alcohol and by the thanks of his grateful patients. He is a scholarly man who knows all about depression and psychosomatic pains in the neck. His own neck still hurts, and it is getting him down.

About twenty years ago, when he was a timid medical student, he opted for a rather pompous manner which involved straightening his neck, pulling his chin down to his throat and occasionally belching—the sort of gentle

belching which is a common form of parlance in aristo-
cratic [English] clubs, preceded by a slight swallowing of
air to provide the necessary ammunition.

A few years later, he refined the head posture to include a deprecatory twist of his head to one side and a
puffing-out of his chest in front. A few years later, he
was making these movements even when he was alone
and sitting quite still: the belching had become a habit,
and in between belching, he tightened his throat and re-
stricted his breathing.

Dr. P had already consulted his psychiatric colleagues
and he had reluctantly cut down on much of his work
since he found it impossible to concentrate. There was
not the remotest possibility of him getting rid of his
neck pain until his strange muscular usages had been
sorted out . . .[1]

"Sorting out" and correcting "strange muscular
usages" initiates many changes in a person. Dr. Moshe
Feldenkrais poses the hypothetical case of someone af-
flicted by hoarseness of the voice (the problem that set
Alexander to work on himself and so led to the evolution of his technique):

Suppose that an actor, speaker, or teacher who has
suffered from hoarseness begins to study ways of improving his enunciation in order to rid himself of his
trouble. He will start by trying to locate the excess effort
he makes in his breathing apparatus and throat. When
he has learned to reduce the expenditure of effort and
to speak more easily, he will note to his surprise that he

---

[1] Wilfred Barlow, *The Alexander Principle* (London: Arrow Books, 1975), p.
12. A somewhat abridged version was published by Alfred A. Knopf, New
York, 1973, entitled *The Alexander Technique*.

has also been doing unnecessary work with the muscles of his jaw and tongue, work of which he was previously unaware and which contributed to his hoarseness. Thus the ease achieved in one area will make closer and more accurate observation possible in related areas.

When he continues to practice his new achievements and can use the muscles of his tongue and jaw without effort, he may discover that he has been using only the back of his mouth and his throat to produce his voice, not the front part of his mouth. This involved a greater effort in breathing because air pressure was needed to force the voice through the mouth. When he learns to use the front of his mouth as well, speaking will have become far easier, and he will discover that there has also been improvement in the use of the muscles of the chest and diaphragm.

He will now discover to his surprise that the interference with the muscles of the chest, diaphragm, and front of the mouth was due to continuous tension in the muscles of the nape of the neck that forced his head and chin forward and distorted his breathing and speaking organs. This will lead him to further discoveries connected with his manner of standing and of moving.

What all this means is that the total personality is involved in proper speech. But even these discoveries, the improvements that they brought about, and the ease of action that resulted are still not the whole story. The man discovers that his voice, previously limited to a single octave, will now reach both considerably higher and lower pitches. He discovers an entirely new quality in his voice and finds that he can sing. This again opens up new possibilities in wider fields and reveals capacities of which he had never dreamed before.[2]

---

[2] Feldenkrais, *Awareness Through Movement*, pp. 88–9.

Use is an elaborate constellation of learned and invented ways of functioning which have become habitual. Some elements of our use are acquired very early and others are added during the course of our life. Some are discarded, some are modified, some become more pronounced, and others retreat into the background. Everyone knows about use to some extent; but few are aware of the intricacy and complexity of the tapestry of interactions.

Nothing is more futile than telling someone to use himself better, which is what we are saying when we tell someone, for instance, to "stand up straight." In response to such an instruction the person may change his way of standing, but his posture will continue to include his many patterns of misuse. The only way to alter use is to give the person repeated experiences of good use—enough so that the nervous system will decide that good use is preferable, then the use pattern will change.

In this book our main emphasis is on the use of the body—which, of course, involves both physical and mental elements. It is at this level of your personal reality that you can achieve the greatest improvement working on your own. We do not ignore or underestimate psychodynamics, which must be included in any total program of reeducation or therapy. But here we stress what you can best do for yourself, and there is much you can do without going into areas where a teacher or therapist should guide the work.

Some Determinants of Use

Our lengthy evolution has not prepared us for the conditions of modern civilized life. In general, the further we depart from a state of nature, the more we are likely to deprive our psychophysical organism of the range of activities it needs to avoid developmental imbalances, crippling distortions, and self-destructive patterns of use. Man in a state of nature is prey to many destructive natural forces, and if we are realistic, we do not envy him his way of life. Nonetheless, he does not misuse himself so badly, or go so counter to his nature, as civilized man.

Man living in a state of nature can do little to protect himself from the natural forces which menace him in so many ways, making his life, in most cases, harsh and brief. Civilized man, however, is in a position to compensate for many of civilization's disadvantages. He could prevent many of the ills he now suffers by ensuring better-balanced development and better use of himself. Psychophysical reeducation could be of great value in producing individuals who are much less self-destructive than almost all of us are at present. If we look at even a few of the ways we go wrong, the importance of good use for both prevention and correction should be quite apparent.

In some important respects, children generally possess greater self-knowledge and awareness than adults. The child is more in touch with his body—his movements, his sensations, his needs, and his desires. He moves and expresses his thoughts and his feelings more freely. His unblunted senses respond to a world that is more colorful and vital, and this perceived reality, in turn, enlivens him. Unless he is intensely involved in action or fantasy, the child is aware of even slight pains and pleasures. The adult fails to perceive, or perceives only dimly, much of what the child senses strongly. By comparison, the adult (and older child) inhibits his responses and expressions of feeling. This might appear desirable, but it is not desirable if, as is typically the case, the inhibition has become automatic and freedom of expression and spontaneity have been lost in the process. Fairly early in life, the child's orientation shifts simultaneously away from the body and toward the external world. Mental processes are now experienced almost as though there were no concomitant changes occurring in the body. There should be an increasing orientation toward the external world, but it need not, and must not, be achieved at the cost of a diluted and distorted awareness of one's own psychophysical reality.

As many have noted, the child's alienation from his body is encouraged when he enters school and is confined for hours each day at his desk, learning to construct a reality shaped very largely by words—a reality increasingly abstract, decreasingly concrete. When countermeasures are not taken to prevent it, concept becomes the enemy of percept. Once the child labels a thing, he assumes that he knows all about it, and so does not explore it any further with the senses, which thus become blunted. This psychogenic impairment furthers the distortion of the senses, especially the kinesthetic sense, which results from misuse of the body.

Even before entering school, however, the child suffers losses of ability which will prevent realization of potential unless they are remedied. For example, one study found that children at the age of two "apparently possessed a degree of physical coordination which by the end of the third year had notably diminished; by the end of the fourth year this coordination had given way to well-established postural habits—rigidly fixed positions of certain parts of the body." [3] From this time onward, but especially after childhood, fewer new movements will be attempted, coordination will continue to diminish, and in many other ways the actualization of body-mind potential will be obstructed. It is thus a necessary task of education to introduce, at the start, work in movement potentials—practical work in the range of bodily movements which are possible. Otherwise, the child will develop inhibitions which will prevent him from even thinking of many of the movements of which he is capable. Such inhibitions will play an important role in impairing the body image and will limit the activities in which the child might engage. Undoubtedly, it will also be conducive to further inhibition of feeling and thinking functions.

Well before he begins his formal schooling, the child may have started to accumulate muscular tensions which he does not release. These tensions may have many causes, including physical injury and pain, mental and emotional distress, and the misguided efforts of

[3] The interested reader should consult the entire article by Alma Frank, "A Study in Infant Development," *Child Development*, Vol. 9 (1938).

adults to hasten the child's development by means of ill-conceived exercises and the encouragement or forcing of premature sitting, standing, or walking. The muscular tensions, as they persist, will affect the way the child moves, his posture, and in time, his sensing of his body. Posture also deteriorates as children imitate adults and other children. Only such deterioration enables the child, for example, to sit slumped for hours in front of a television set or at a school desk. In a well-organized body with unimpaired awareness, such a position would be too painful. That it is not demonstrates all too clearly that damage has been done to the musculoskeletal system and the self-sensing apparatus.

Despite these early changes for the worse, the child, as compared to the youth or adult, remains free and mobile and much more aware of his body. Since the child is in close contact with his body, he knows when something is amiss and expresses his feelings. However, a great many of his distress signals are overlooked, misinterpreted, actively discouraged, or even punished. Thus, the child learns to inhibit further, first the expression of his feelings, and then the feelings themselves. If he learns to ignore certain muscular tensions, and later to inhibit his consciousness of them, then gradually those mechanisms by which the body signals to the brain what the muscles are doing become seriously impaired. Faulty use should be clearly sensed so that the body can begin to correct itself, but, with prolonged and habitual misuse, the faulty actions come to feel "right" and the correct ones feel "wrong." The kinesthetic sense is distorted, and the awareness of the body deteriorates, so that body and body image increasingly cease to coincide. Poor use of the body, with sensory distortions and unconscious chronic muscular contractions, begins to deform the body symmetry and to displace the skeleton. Faulty breathing, which saps vitality and stamina and impairs a variety of functions, is likely to result, in turn creating emotional and psychological problems, learning disabilities, and so on. We speak here not of exceptional cases, but of what is typical, although there are, of course, great differences in degree.

Dr. Wilfred Barlow reports that already by the age of eleven

> 70 percent of all boys and girls show quite marked muscular and postural deficiencies. Mostly these defects appear as passing inefficiencies and difficulties in learning; they become accentuated in emotional situations, and they presage an uneasy adolescence in which childhood faults become blown up into full-fledged defects. By the age of eighteen, only 5 percent of the population are free from defects, 15 percent have slight defects, 65 percent have quite severe defects, and 15 percent have very severe defects. These figures are based on my published surveys of boys and girls from secondary schools, and students from physical training, music and drama colleges, some of whom might reasonably be expected to have a higher physical standard than the rest of the population. It is almost certain that you, the reader . . . have quite pronounced defects of which you yourself are unconscious, and which your doctors, teachers, or parents did not notice, or did not worry about, or just accepted as an inevitable part of the way you are made.[4]

---

[4] Barlow, *The Alexander Principle*, p. 15.

Barlow is speaking here of English children, but he has participated in a world survey of physical training systems and finds that also in the United States, Australia, and the Soviet Union, for example, the problems are the same, since conventional physical education fails everywhere to "leave its pupils with either the knowledge or the desire to maintain healthful activity in advancing years." He adds: "The evidence now is quite incontrovertible. We are witnessing a widespread deterioration in USE which begins at an early age, and which present educational methods are doing little to prevent. Most people have lost good USE by the time they are past early childhood. Not all the time, but in most of their activities and while they are resting. Nobody bothers about it because nobody notices until the defects have become severe."[5]

Our own observations of children and young people in the United States and other countries fully support Barlow's unhappy findings. We have also found that even defects which appear glaring to the educated observer go unrecognized by doctors, school nurses, physical education instructors, and others who could initiate remedial action. Only when there is a serious breakdown of functioning or when some familiar pathology is present do these health authorities perceive that the situation urgently needs to be corrected. *What is wrong must be more wrong than the norm* if they are to perceive it. But the norm itself is already very, very wrong—wrong enough for 80 percent of youths, at

[5] Barlow, *The Alexander Principle*, pp. 155–6.

eighteen years of age, to be found to have severe defects.

When we consider what has already been said, we may begin to have some new insights into the causes of many so-called symptoms of aging. Many are simply symptoms of "bad use," and one proof of this contention is the fact that when even quite elderly people are taught good use, many of the "symptoms of aging" decrease in severity or disappear altogether. If these were truly symptoms of aging, then they would be irreversible by any means which are presently available.

There are ways of using the body which are efficient and conducive to health. There are other ways of using the body which are inefficient, wasteful of strength and energy, and otherwise detrimental to health and to well-being in general. How we use our organism affects us more profoundly and totally than any other single factor (excluding some extraordinarily crippling disaster). But good use, which ought to be basic, is a concept little or not at all known to those responsible for our education and health. We should consider what these authorities do offer, and whether it furthers good use or misuse, whether it helps us or harms us, and how much real understanding of the body-mind underlies the prevailing approaches to physical training and fitness.

Conventional Approaches

There is a "New Physical Education," with philosophy and methods superior to the old, and we applaud the improvement while hoping that it will incorporate more of the understanding and methods in this book and in the writings of Alexander and, still more importantly, Feldenkrais. Then the needed reforms will be achieved even sooner and will be more comprehensive.

The average person, however, if he wishes to improve his body—which he separates from his mind in contemplating such a goal—is still at the mercy of books and magazine articles and teachers who offer him "exercise programs" of limited value and almost unlimited tedium. Choice examples are the official fitness programs of the President's Council on Physical Fitness and the Royal Canadian Air Force. These consist of mechanically and mindlessly repeated movements aimed at strengthening and stretching the muscles and improving the respiratory and circulatory systems. If one is able to persist long enough, they will be of some benefit in increasing strength, stamina, and suppleness. They will strengthen everything, including the defects; they will not contribute significantly to improving use or to correcting the body image or the faulty sensory mechanisms which are at the root of so many of our personal problems, both mental and physical. Dr. Wilfred Barlow has studied the effects of a year's pursuit of typical "stretch and strengthen" exercises and physiotherapy programs on students. Among his findings: increased postural defects at the end of the year.

Running and jogging, weightlifting, rope-skipping, swimming, isometrics, isotonics, and sports in general also do little or nothing to improve use, and are in various ways detrimental, although most of them afford some benefits and, for the majority of people, are better than nothing. Dedicated runners and weightlifters, in particular, may derive great emotional rewards as well as physical benefits. However, they frequently injure themselves, which they would be unlikely to do if mind and body were better integrated and their sensing more accurate.

Sports and athletics are not the best road to health or improved bodily functioning. Those who enjoy them should engage in them for whatever rewards they offer, but they should also be aware of some of the disadvantages. For example:

> There is hardly any form of athletics in which all of the muscles are not brought into play, but when we study their activities we see that some parts of the body are taxed sufficiently to produce considerable development while others are only slightly used. Marvelous control is required in some parts to execute the movements, while others require little or no control. Every game or sport exercises and develops some groups of muscles or some region of the body more than other groups or regions and in time produces more or less deformity if not counter-balanced by other features of the exercise program. The unevenness in the distribution of effort results in uneven development and control. The result is that our athletes are miserable specimens.[6]

The unbalanced development resulting from athletics can only be compensated for by remedial exer-

[6] Herbert Shelton, *Exercise!* (Chicago: Natural Hygiene Press, 1971), p. 37.

cise. However, that is not something that the average person can do for himself; he would need the services of a skilled teacher to direct his efforts. Most people who exercise, with or without a teacher, do not achieve what they hope to. Many with protruding abdomens, for instance, think it logical to embark on a program of sit-ups. But since the protrusion is caused by contractions in the muscles of the back and by bad posture, all they achieve is strong muscles in a still-protruding abdomen.

> Practically without exception, athletes (and dancers) deform their bodies, sometimes monstrously, because they have only partial awareness of them. Since they don't understand the interdependence of their muscles and their antagonists, since they don't use the muscles that are best suited to the effort they want to make, they take their strength where they find it first. By forcing themselves, they have no choice, they're forced to hurt themselves. But forcing oneself, surpassing oneself, are often the rules of the game. Even when his goal is to beat his rival, an athlete out to win can rarely avoid "beating," which is to say "punishing," himself.[7]

The athlete lacks a sufficiently thorough and applicable knowledge of body mechanics and of use, and his sensory mechanisms, too, are distorted, as are almost everyone's. Thus, when his sport calls for violent action, he is especially prone to injury, more often self-inflicted than inflicted by opponents. (We are speaking of accidental injuries; other damage is inherent in the sport itself.)

[7] Thérèse Bertherat and Carol Bernstein, *The Body Has Its Reasons* (New York: Pantheon Books, 1977), pp. 59–60.

Some athletes have massively developed upper bodies, but comparatively undeveloped legs. Others, like many dancers, have upper bodies so poorly developed in comparison to the lower body that they seem to have made anatomical freaks of themselves. Two activities often thought to be especially beneficial are swimming and cycling. Bertherat notes, however, that swimming typically has the effect of further developing back muscles which are already overdeveloped, so that there is a consequent underdevelopment of the front of the body—a combination that thwarts good use of the body and is harmful in many specific ways as well as in general. Professional swimmers often suffer from such overdevelopment of the dorsal muscle and such contraction that the skeleton is displaced. She writes that a common effect of cycling is a "tightening of the muscles in the back of the neck and lower back; on the other hand, a loss of tonicity in the abdominal muscles and a compression of the stomach . . . can lead to digestive problems (very common in professional cyclists)."[8] Cycling also tends to pull the shoulders forward, cramp the chest, and overdevelop the extensors of the thigh, according to Shelton, who provides a catalog of the damaging effects of many sports. Particularly detrimental, he says, are one-sided sports, such as putting the shot. If the shot-putter also works with the discus, javelin, and hammer, the results are even worse: ". . . the person who has specialized in the shot-put a few years will be found to be deformed. The most pronounced fault [when the person is right-

[8] Bertherat and Bernstein, *The Body Has Its Reasons*, pp. 58–9.

handed] is a curvature of the spine with its convexity to the right. His right arm is larger and longer than the left and there is often a difference in the legs." Jumping, hurdling, and especially pole vaulting also develop one side much more than the other.[9]

How many people taking up a sport are given information about the deformities likely to result? How many are offered remedial exercise programs? The objection to these asymmetries and imbalances is by no means just esthetic. Not only do they affect body use, which affects functioning, they may eventually result in crippling conditions—back pain, rheumatism, and so on.

Participation in sports when it is not continued into later life makes no notable contribution to either health or longevity in the vast majority of cases. Many kinds of regular exercise will defer some of the symptoms of aging and lengthen life, especially when they strengthen the cardiovascular system. They will also reinforce defects, as we have noted. Their worst effect is to undermine the motivation of the person to care for himself. Not very many people are disciplined enough to maintain a lifelong program of exercise which they do not enjoy. Psychophysical Reeducation differs from these methods in that it establishes a pattern of good use which eventually becomes self-sustaining. With the exercises presented in this book, an individual should be able to continue to work by himself. Even if he does not, his improved use is likely to be retained; will mark-

[9] Shelton, *Exercise!*, pp. 42–3.

edly benefit his health and his functioning in general, and should enable him to live better and longer.

Dr. Wilfred Barlow has kept track of the Alexander teachers in England, all of them thoroughly trained in good use. He has come up with a statistic which, to our knowledge, is unique, and which illustrates as well as anything can the importance of what we have been discussing:

> Since Alexander started working seventy-five years ago when he was 30, more than one hundred teachers of his method have been trained in this country. Of these [teachers in England], only four have died, including Alexander himself, aged 87, and his first assistant, Ethel Webb, aged 94: no coronaries, no cancers, no strokes, no rheumatoid arthritis, no discs, no ulcers, no neurological disorders, no severe mental disorders, just occasionally some rather unlikely behavior; accidents inevitably, but recovery to good functioning and no accident-proneness. By and large, a standard of day-to-day health and happiness which most people encounter only in their earliest years.[10]

---

[10] Barlow, *The Alexander Principle*, p. 10.

The Shaping and Reshaping of People

THE POTENTIAL HEIGHT of a person is limited by the length of the skeleton. The actual height of most people, however, is rarely all that the bones would allow. The body is shorter than it might be because of various skeletal deformities—curvature of the spine most notably—which are produced by muscular tensions and poor posture. The typical adult body will increase in height by up to two inches when the muscles are freed from superfluous tensions and the skeleton is allowed to resume what should be its normal extension.

Muscular contractions not only shorten the body, they also displace the skeletal parts in a variety of ways, which differ from one person to the next. The joints are often compressed on one side and drawn apart on the other. Eventually the cartilage between the joints may be worn away, so that the bones grind against each other and suffer damage. Some muscular tensions, of course, are normal and necessary—without them the body would collapse in a heap, as a skeleton does when it has no support. As a general rule, the healthy person should be unaware of these muscular tensions, but aware of the abnormal and unnecessary ones. Who wants to be constantly aware, for example, of the muscular tensions in the neck which are required for the support of the head? Or of the muscular effort needed to keep the lower jaw from hanging slack? When standing, the legs must make an effort, easily verified by comparing the differences between the calves when standing, sitting, and lying. Superfluous tensions, on the other hand, should be sensed as soon as they occur so that they can be eliminated.

It is the muscles which determine the body's form; thus, the form of the body is not fixed but changeable. Françoise Mézières, a French "revolutionary" in the field of physiotherapy, describes herself as a sculptor of living bodies. She holds—and proves in practice— that even hereditary "morphological types" and ac- quired deformities are not irreversible (except when resulting from fractures and mutilations). She teaches her students that "the only normal morphology is that which corresponds to the relation of the proportions of the body's parts to one another that characterizes Greek art of the classical period. This art was unique in representing the human being as he *should be*—that is to say, as he could be if he could give reality to his true potential. . . . [She teaches her students] not to accept any treatment that is not directed toward that perfect form. For neither the importance of the subject's deformation nor his age prevent him from being able to approach that form in an appreciable way."[1] The bodies of the elderly are no exception and may be even more malleable than those of the young.

The extraordinary malleability of the human body has been confirmed many times over by practitioners of the Alexander Technique and of Feldenkrais' system of Functional Integration and by the authors, among others. It is because of this malleability that the body can be so badly distorted by use, by emotional and other stresses, and by the person's self-image.

Feldenkrais writes:

> Many of our failings, physical and mental, need not therefore be considered as diseases to be cured, nor an unfortunate trait of character, for they are neither. They are an acquired result of a learned faulty mode of doing. The body only executes what the nervous system makes it do. It moulds itself during growth for a longer period, and to a greater extent, than in any other animal. Actions repeated innumerable times for years on end, such as all our habitual actions, mould even the bones, let alone the muscular envelope. The physical faults that appear in our body long after we were born are mainly the result of activity we have imposed on it. Faulty modes of standing and walking produce flat feet, and it is the mode of standing and walking that must be corrected, and not the feet. The extent to which our

[1] Bertherat and Bernstein, *The Body Has Its Reasons,* pp. 78-9.

frame is able to adjust itself to the use and requirements we make of it seems to be limitless; by learning a better use of control, the feet, the eyes, or whatever organ it may be, will again adjust themselves and change their shape and function accordingly. The transformations that can be produced, and their rapidity, sometimes border on the incredible.[2]

According to Feldenkrais, reeducation can "rebuild the entire frame."

Most large changes in the form and functions of the body occur as a result of habitual actions which are repeated "innumerable times for years on end." However, we have also observed muscle tensions in response to emotional stress which are extreme enough to deform the appearance of the body almost instantly, even displacing the skeleton. For example, one shoulder may become elevated and twisted to the side, with consequent changes in the neck, the rib cage, etc. Such emotional traumatizing of the body-mind can create a conditioned response to similar but lesser stresses in the future, so that the deformation soon becomes permanent unless remedial measures are taken.

Similarly, body deformations, even when they have existed for years, can be very quickly removed by a skilled practitioner working on the body with his hands. Feldenkrais, for example, has countless times demonstrated his ability to straighten out badly humped backs, severely curved spines, and numerous

[2] Moshe Feldenkrais, *Body and Mature Behavior* (New York: International Universities Press, 1970), p. 152.

other deformities, some of them almost lifelong. He does it in twenty to thirty minutes of work, and to the onlooker the results appear almost miraculous. The treatment of severe conditions must be repeated in order to effect permanent change, the number of treatments required depending on age, the length of time the condition has existed, the degree of severity, and other factors. Sometimes even a single session suffices to free and restore to use some part of the body which has been immobilized for years. In our own experience, when someone's body has been appropriately worked on for a time, one begins to sense that the body has become extraordinarily malleable and that the nervous system is now ready to accept change. When this occurs, the muscles no longer obstruct the effort, and one can, as it were, rearrange parts of the skeleton, effectively reshaping the body. There is an element of the uncanny in one's feeling that the body being worked with has become almost like clay or putty. As Feldenkrais remarks above, "The transformations that can be produced, and their rapidity, sometimes border on the incredible." How is it that such changes are possible?

Organization of the muscles and voluntary movements can occur only after the prerequisite changes have taken place in the motor cortex of the brain. When there is extensive inhibition in the motor cortex, one cannot perform voluntary actions. When the inhibition is partial, one cannot move the corresponding parts.

When, for example, a wrist is broken, and is then

prevented from moving by means of a splint or some other device, then there may occur an inhibition in the motor cortex which prevents movement of the wrist. Later, the broken wrist heals and could move, but the inhibition in the motor cortex persists. Only when the inhibition is lifted by some means will the person find that he can again move his wrist.

There are many methods which may prove effective in achieving the desired disinhibition. The physiotherapist, who very often has no accurate formulation of the problem, nonetheless may succeed by massaging and moving the wrist, inducing sensations of hot and cold, applying electrical stimulation, and so on, while continually exhorting the patient to move his wrist. A psychic or faith healer may achieve almost instantaneous disinhibition by means of a powerful emotional appeal or simply because the person has great faith in his powers. Hypnosis may succeed through a heightened suggestibility coupled with various sorts of suggestions. Many "miracle cures" can be understood as successful appeals to the brain to alter body functioning. What remains mysterious is just why some individuals do and some do not respond to the different approaches.

Obviously, very rapid and extensive changes in a human body are produced by some extraordinary change in the brain which in turn affects the body, so that paralyzed limbs can move, vision can improve dramatically, normal speech can be restored, and so on. There are cancer remissions which occur when an individual is confronted with a sudden life-threatening sit-

uation, such as an auto collision. At Lourdes and other
healing shrines, people who have been doubled over
and in agony for years suddenly stand erect and walk
away free from pain. These are not tall tales but well-
verified instances of dramatic changes in the body's
condition which we must consider to be triggered by
prior changes in the brain. Any bodily organ could
probably be substantially altered if only the appropriate brain action could be induced. It would seem that
only truly congenital conditions or those which result
from accidental or surgical mutilation of the body cannot be remedied in this manner.

The easiest access appears to be through the motor
cortex to the muscles, possibly because a high degree
of awareness of the musculoskeletal system is natural to
man, however much of it he may lose as he continues
through life. Those organs and processes of which one
is not naturally so aware are more difficult to change,
especially in a more or less permanent way. However,
it is not impossible. In replicated experiments, hypnosis has been used to substantially enlarge female
breasts. Given such a fact, it would seem perfectly possible to enlarge or diminish internal organs and other
body parts. Certainly we know from yoga, autogenic
training, biofeedback, and many other sources, that it
is possible to take voluntary control of "involuntary"
processes. Later, we will discuss certain ways of utilizing mind-body interactions which can be applied as
self-healing techniques or just for more effective living.

The body-mind is malleable, then, not only in its
form but also in many if not all its functions. The

changes which can be produced may be great as well as small, and they include mental as well as physical changes, so that the whole being of the individual is well within the scope of self-regulation and self-improvement.

Among other things, Psychophysical Reeducation is a neural reeducation which makes the nervous system demonstrably more responsive and amenable to change. Psychophysical exercises are in part effective communications to the brain, specifying bodily changes which the brain can and will effect in response to the appropriate stimulus.

The Mind, the Brain, and the Body

WE ARE NO MORE ABLE than anyone else to resolve the "mind-brain problem": Are mind and brain two separate systems, or is mind-brain a single system? Is the mind "explained" by the brain? In the absence of a final conclusion, it seems to be more practically useful to treat the mind and the brain as separate elements, semi-independent but interactive at every conscious moment (and perhaps unconscious as well).

In his remarkable book *The Mystery of the Mind,* Dr. Wilder Penfield summed up a lifetime of work as a neurosurgeon and brain researcher by concluding that the mind does appear to be a separate system or element with its own energy. Quoting the ancient Hippocratic insight, voiced at a time when consciousness was almost universally thought to reside in the heart, that "the brain is messenger" to, and "the interpreter of," consciousness, Penfield gives a modern version: "the brain's highest mechanism is as 'messenger' between the mind and the other mechanisms of the brain."[1] This coincides with a line of thinking that the authors have been pursuing for some time.

We picture the brain as a biocomputer which can be controlled by the mind, although often it is not. Most of what is often thought of as the "unconscious mind" and its processes would then be seen as the computer-brain in action. This activity is based on built-in evolutionary programming, on the one hand, and programming by experience, on the other. Programming by experience is more important in human than in lower animal life, since a larger part of the human brain is "uncommitted" at birth and so remains open to programming by our experiences in later life. Unlike the brain, the element of mind cannot be (or has not been) localized or measured. Like electricity, it can be known only through its manifestations.

The computer-brain—by which we mean the brain excluding its highest mechanism—"runs" the body according to its own programs, except when the mind is controlling it. This would explain why, as Gurdjieff, Alexander, Feldenkrais, and others have put it, ordinary human consciousness more nearly resembles sleep than true wakefulness or awareness. This is why the human being is typically more automaton than au-

[1] Wilder Penfield, *The Mystery of the Mind* (Princeton: Princeton University Press, 1975). The quotation given in this paragraph is found on page 46.

tonomous, although he has the potential to be free. To the extent that there is awareness, the mind is in control of the brain. This awareness is always partial, for even when the mind *is* controlling the brain, many internal processes continue to be organized or directed by the computer, which presumably has regulatory and organizational control of the entire body. If this is true, then the whole body can be approached and directed through the computer if we learn to program it with the mind.

The extraordinary functioning exhibited by hypnotic subjects and yogis, for example, supports the belief that the body can be altered in almost any way whatsoever if only the brain can be made to accept the suggestions or instructions given it. The body appears to be merely a performer, acting out whatever is organized or directed by the brain.

In hypnosis, psychoanalysis, and other procedures, an effort is made to communicate with the unconscious mind, since it has been observed that there is "something" within us that can achieve a good deal which the conscious mind cannot (without long and rigorous training in psychophysical or "mind control" disciplines). The unconscious mind has access to, or partly consists of, symbolic processes which can only be known by making the unconscious conscious. It has access to memories which the conscious mind cannot retrieve except with its help. It can control involuntary bodily processes; heal us or make us sick; accelerate or decelerate mental processes, thus seeming to distort time; regulate the sensations of pain and pleasure; and

perform a great array of other feats which are little understood. The unconscious would seem to contain sub-
personalities, some more intelligent, wiser, and more
learned than the conscious personality itself.

However, the notion of an unconscious mind is really unnecessary to explain these phenomena as long as
we concede that the brain has direct access to the body
and to many latent capacities to which the conscious
mind ordinarily does not. These capacities can, of
course, be stimulated by drugs or by chemical changes
originating in the brain itself. Hypnosis could be seen
as a means of partially bypassing the mind in order to
approach the brain biocomputer directly, or alterna-
tively as a way of increasing the mind's ability to control the brain. However, in recent years much evidence
has emerged that effective controls over the body and
its functions can be established without inducing a
trance, or administering drugs.

The conscious mind appears more and more to have
a far greater potential than used to be supposed. This
does not mean that altered states of consciousness have
no value in facilitating bodily changes; the evidence is
overwhelming that profound changes in the body can
occur when consciousness is altered, especially if altered profoundly. But there seems to be another, less
well explored way: training the body to respond to instructions issued by the conscious mind. Of these two
approaches, the second would seem to be the more re-
liable and the more desirable, since conscious control
strengthens awareness and the conscious mind. On
the other hand, the use of mind-altering techniques

has often been criticized because these appear to strengthen the brain-computer.

The Body and Experience

The living body is always changing. All experience alters the body in some way, producing electrical, chemical, glandular, muscular, and many other kinds of changes. The more complex the body and its nervous system, the greater the range of possible changes. In the case of human beings, the continuous flux of our bodies is more or less unconscious, depending upon the extent of our awareness, but always unconscious to some extent. In general, we are aware of changes which are gross, and unaware of changes which are more subtle.

Movements, sensations, thoughts, and emotions all engender bodily changes of varying magnitude and intensity. Many animals visibly respond in a variety of ways to sensations and emotions and, no doubt, to thoughts as well. (The notion that animals do not think is quickly losing credibility—it is nothing but a general human conceit and a specific "scientific" one.) Dogs cringe at harsh words, angry voices, and even negative attitudes, just as people do, and in time their use of themselves is affected if they are abused sufficiently. Like humans, they can accumulate muscular tensions to the point that the skeleton is displaced, the joints stiffen, movement—including breathing—is impaired, the dog becomes stupid and chronically anxious, and his eyes and facial expression allow the whole world to read his misery. Of course such outward manifestations have many counterpart internal phenomena; the total organism is involved.

When we are frightened the muscles are tensed, breathing and heart rate are altered, the ability to think clearly is impaired, and the endocrine system does not function properly. If we are frequently or chronically frightened, anxious or otherwise emotionally disturbed, then the accompanying bodily changes are chronic. In time, such a condition is likely to produce other serious physical (and mental) symptoms, which may even kill us. On the other hand, serenity and happiness protect us, not completely, but to a considerable extent.

In this book we have included exercises which will demonstrate to you clearly that emotions, images, and words can be used to effect rapid and far-reaching changes in the body. Obviously, if an exercise produces such changes, so does experience in general. It is important to understand these mind-brain-body interactions, and to recognize the possibility of using them to better determine your life.

Thinking about or imagining an action immediately prepares the muscles to carry it out. If you merely think about making a fist, for example, then the muscles will measurably begin to organize as they would if you were actually clenching your fist. The body's response is all the greater when the imagined action is emotionally charged. Thinking about food will elicit salivation, especially if the taste, aroma, texture, and

appearance of the food are imagined. Vivid sexual fantasies will readily induce tumescence in the sexual
organs. On the other hand, if there is sufficient conflict
between the brain-computer and the mind, then even
the strongest sexual stimulation and the liveliest desire
may not be able to override the inhibitions, which set
up effective countertendencies in the body, making
performance impossible. In either case, the fantasy
and the emotions it produces trigger changes in the
body which include the muscles, the glands, the blood
flow, and much more. The exercises in this book also
demonstrate that the brain issues instructions to the
body in a language which the untutored conscious
mind does not know, and alters the body in ways which
are predictable only to someone who understands that
language. The exercises will enable you to "speak to
the brain" directly, yielding results which the conscious
mind could not have anticipated.

Methods and Techniques

It has been known since the most ancient times that
both images and words can be deliberately used to alter
the condition of one's own body or the body of another
person. Men long ago learned to use sound, touch, and
movement to effect changes in their bodies. By these
means, they apprised the brain of their wishes, whatever they may have thought they were doing. A great
variety of approaches can yield similar results, for example in the case of healing. It is the brain which

heals; the various approaches are ways of communicating with it, and the success of the approach may depend upon what the mind believes, how the brain has been previously programmed, the emotional intensity produced, and other factors. Some methods may serve to "bracket" the mind, preventing its beliefs from interfering; others may give the mind greater control over the body. The following discussion is limited to uses of images and words to bring about bodily changes. We will also confine ourselves to methods currently in use in various therapies and methods of re-education.

In Europe, many thousands of persons have been treated for a great variety of physical and mental problems with what is called autogenic training, a discipline which has its roots in hypnosis as well as yoga and other Eastern psychophysical methods. In autogenic training, a person daily practices giving different kinds of verbal commands or instructions to his body until the body is trained to respond to almost any command that is given it. At first, for example, the student might instruct his right arm and hand to feel heavy and warm. After a few sessions during which these instructions are repeated, the arm actually begins to feel heavy and warm. After that, other parts of the body are similarly trained and eventually even normally involuntary processes such as the heartbeat and blood flow can be regulated by the student's verbal instructions. Visual and other sensory imageries are sometimes used to achieve changes in bodily, emotional, and mental states, but autogenic training emphasizes verbal control. The practical limits of this method of self-regulation have not yet been established, but there are indications that almost any possible change could be effected if only the proper formulation of instructions could be discovered.

The technique developed by Alexander also involves establishing verbal controls over bodily responses. A teacher, working with his hands, provides the sensations and organization of the body while the student translates the sensations he is experiencing into verbal commands. For example, the teacher might place his hands on the student's neck and raise him from a sitting to a standing position, releasing and lengthening the neck while also positioning the head. The student articulates the accompanying sensations as "neck releasing and lengthening, head forward and up," or something of the sort. In time the neck and head will respond to the verbal commands alone. This allows the student to work on himself, until the "good use" becomes habitual.

The "pure" Alexander Technique employs only explicit verbal instructions, carefully and repeatedly linked to particular sensations through the joint efforts of student and instructor. Images are avoided as a likely source of error. This is not to say, however, that images are ineffective in changing the body. Imagery can be an extremely powerful tool for effecting such changes, even when used by an untrained person. In his book *The Mind of a Mnemonist*,[2] the Russian psychol-

[2] A. R. Luria, *The Mind of a Mnemonist*, trans. Lynn Solotaroff (New York: Basic Books, tr. 1968).

ogist A. R. Luria describes the case of a patient whose natural sensitivity to visual and other images was extraordinarily well developed. The man was able to change the temperature of his hands, for example, merely by imagining that he had thrust one hand into ice water while holding the other close to a flame. Luria's patient performed many other feats of this sort, which usually can only be achieved by yogis and adepts in similar disciplines after long and arduous training.

Working with hypnosis, Milton H. Erickson and others, including the authors, have demonstrated not only the numerous changes in the body which occur in response to images and words but also that images can be used to greatly accelerate the body's learning. One of the brain's capacities is to accelerate in such a way that imagery can be experienced within brief amounts of clock-measured time which subjectively seem to be much longer in duration. For instance, someone who has previously seen a film that lasted for two hours on the screen is enabled in trance to see it again in its entirety in only a minute or even less of clock-measured time. That minute of clock time will be experienced subjectively as the two hours which were originally required to see the film. The images are experienced as moving at a normal rate. This phenomenon of imagery and "time distortion" is not limited in its application to material that has been experienced before and is merely reproduced, as in the case of the film. One can, for example, use it to experience practicing piano, playing golf, or whatever. At the end of a minute of clock time, experienced subjectively as an hour at practice, the improvement will be indistinguishable from improvement achieved by practicing objectively (with the body) for the longer period of time. Or, sometimes, the improvement is greater when the practice is done in this way. The method has been demonstrated repeatedly and the results would seem to rest partially upon the fact that at a minuscule level the body always organizes itself and in some sense carries out whatever action is imaged.

In a series of studies in ideokinesis, the late Lulu Sweigard demonstrated that the body will even spontaneously imitate an image perceived external to itself. For instance, she used the well-known illustration of Alice in Wonderland with a greatly elongated neck to make students aware that they responded to that drawing by unconsciously lengthening their own necks. Other examples of imitative bodily responses to external images were shown as well and raise the question of the extent to which such imitation is a significant factor in the lives of some or all of us.

In the Feldenkrais Method, Awareness Through Movement, kinesthetic imagery is linked to sensations of movement and this imagery then is used to quickly and easily transfer learning from one side of the body to the other. For example, many movements of the left shoulder are done, the shoulder becoming increasingly free while the student focuses attention on the movements and accompanying sensations. When the student can clearly image kinesthetically the movements and sensations, he then imagines doing the same movements with the right shoulder. Then, in a comparatively brief amount of time, usually a few minutes, he achieves the same or greater freedom in the right shoulder joint that he achieved by perhaps forty-five minutes of movements on the left side.

Several of the techniques we have mentioned strongly emphasize maintaining as precise and well-defined a connection as possible between the image or verbal command and the associated bodily effect. The Alexander and Feldenkrais systems both provide their students with considerable experience in keying words or images to the appropriate movements and sensations. Other approaches, such as autogenic training, rely on the ability of the unconscious mind or some form of body intelligence to respond "correctly" to verbal instructions, repeated again and again as the body becomes increasingly responsive. Hypnosis similarly relies on the subject's unconscious mind to transmit the hypnotist's suggestions to the body. Other techniques use images which are clearly (or not so clearly) symbolic; sometimes it is difficult to tell whether one is working with a real symbol system or with representational images which elicit literal responses.

Several physicians, the best known of whom is the radiologist Carl Simonton, have reported some success in treating malignant tumors with a combination of hypnosis or relaxation, imagery, and, in Simonton's case, radiation therapy. Psychotherapy and counseling are also available to help cancer patients modify certain mental and emotional attitudes which, characteristically, are often already present long before the cancer is detected. Some of the imagery used in these sessions is representational: Three times daily, the patient visualizes the cancer and his white blood cells fighting the disease. Or the imagery may be symbolic: The patient is encouraged to visualize, say, some animal which represents the cancer, then another, more powerful animal, which attacks and tries to destroy the cancer symbol. The authors are familiar with a case in which a group of psychiatrists and other physicians administered LSD to a patient, who concentrated for hours on an image of his tumor shrinking, until at last it vanished. Subsequently it was discovered that the tumor had actually disappeared. In several cases, we have used hypnosis and imagery techniques to treat breast tumors, which vanished after a few sessions. There was no way of knowing whether these tumors were malignant, since these patients were all spared the painful necessity of a biopsy. Less dramatically, warts and rashes can easily be made to appear and disappear by hypnotic suggestion; some subjects have raised blisters on their skin by concentrating strongly on an image of themselves holding a hand near a flame. In all these cases, it is the images themselves which elicit the changes in the body. Hypnosis helps to intensify the images, but someone whose powers of imagination are exceptionally well developed can bring about the same changes without hypnosis.

The brain can produce small or quite extensive changes in the body, instantaneously or over long periods, and is in fact doing so all the time, whether consciously or unconsciously, in response to experiences originating inside or outside the body. These transforming experiences include our emotions, words, and images; if we can use these to communicate directly with the brain, then the mind will truly control the body. Otherwise, the body will be directed only by the brain-computer according to its inherited and acquired programs. The vital interaction of the mind and the brain-computer will remain beyond our ken and beyond our control.

An Introduction to Yourself

ALL SYSTEMS for developing human potential try to teach us to know and understand ourselves better. But most of these demand a kind of blind, unquestioning faith, however vigorously they might deny it, and teach ways of thinking and feeling which inevitably reflect the methods and objectives of the particular system. Psychophysical Reeducation attempts to introduce you to yourself as you are, and to inform you of certain facts about yourself and ways in which you can change them for the better if you wish. Its demonstrations are experiential, so that you become directly aware of your situation, and of changes in that situation. As far as possible, reeducation avoids persuasion or suggestion; you need never take anything on faith. However, it is strictly impossible to teach or demonstrate anything "purely," without a hint of persuasion or suggestion. All we can do is reduce this interference to a minimum, so that your experiences will be as much your own as possible. The primary objective of the psychophysical method is not better health, better use, or longer life, although all these are obviously important. The primary objective is *freedom*.

In this chapter, we will illustrate in greater detail than we have before some of the ways in which you are obstructing yourself, preventing yourself from realizing your potential, from being truly free. The exercises presented in the following chapters will reveal some of this undeveloped potential to you, pointing the way to further discovery and establishing a momentum that will allow you to continue on your own.

To begin, think about what you would be doing if, instead of sitting or lying down and reading, you were walking around the room. Take an imaginary walk around the room, going back and forth several times, trying to notice what you do while you are walking. Put the book down and do it now in your imagination.

When you have done that, return in your imagination to your actual position, sitting or lying down. Reconstruct what you did as you walked around the room in your imagination. Take a little time to do that.

Now consider the following: When you got up, what did you do? When you started walking, which foot took the first step? When you turned, did you turn to the left or to the right, or perhaps to the left on one occasion, to the right on another? Whatever you did, it will have been the same as what you normally do when you walk.

While the left foot and leg were going forward, what were you doing with the left arm? As you were walking, what part of your foot made contact with the floor first, and what part left the floor last?

It should not be difficult to imagine an activity as familiar as walking, and to attend to what is being imagined. If it is, try physically getting up and walking around the room a few times, paying close attention to your movements and your sensations, then returning to your present position. Please do this before reading any further.

Now that you have returned, recollect what you did in getting up from your chair (or your couch, or whatever). Did you use one or both arms to help you, how did you use them, and did you use first one and then the other, or one more than the other? Did you push down harder with one foot and, if so, which one? As you walked, what were the feelings in the ankles, the knees, the hip joints, the shoulder joints? How extensive were the movements in the joints? How freely did your arms swing? Did you notice this time which arm goes forward with which leg? Did you notice what direction you turned in, and what you did with your hands and arms, your shoulders, your neck and head, and your eyes, when you turned? Were you aware of your breathing, whether it was free or whether you held your breath as you tried to concentrate on your movements? Were you, until now, aware of your breathing as you tried to answer these questions? As you observed your movements while walking, did it seem to you that you were walking as you usually do, or did you begin to wonder whether you were doing some things differently?

Are you aware right now (without making an effort) of whether your feet and your arms exert equal or different pressures on the surfaces they are resting on? Are you aware, without checking, of your spine, including your neck, where it curves and the different ways it is curving, whether it curves at all? We could ask you a hundred additional questions, rather few of which you would be able to answer if you are as lacking in awareness as the great majority of people.

The efforts you have just made were of three kinds. The first was to imagine an activity and then to recall what it was that you imagined. In this case, your imagination and memory could be no better than your customary awareness of what you do while walking. Secondly, you were asked to physically walk around the room, paying close attention to yourself, and then to examine what it was that you observed. This also involved some recollection. Thirdly, you were asked about your current awareness, so that no recollection was called for. All three efforts should be simple enough, but there are reasons why they are not, and you should know more about those reasons.

Therefore, please stand for a while as you normally do, with your arms hanging at your sides. Be aware of whether your knees are locked or whether they are very slightly flexed, and ask yourself whether you normally stand with the knees locked or a little flexed. In a well-organized body the knees will not be locked.

Note how your hands are hanging and whether the backs of the hands are facing forward or to the sides. If they face to the sides then something has occurred to alter the natural position of the shoulder joints. No doubt there is excessive tension in the muscles of the back. Many people stand with the palms against the thighs and the backs of the hands facing out to the sides. This is a requisite of military posture, which also requires that the chest be thrust out and the shoulders thrown back, thus curving the spine and pushing the pelvis forward. As was once pointed out to the British army, such a posture may in time produce respiratory and cardiovascular disorders, arthritis, and other problems.

With a few people, including some regressed schizophrenics, the distortion in the shoulder joints is so great that they actually stand with the palms of the hands facing out to the sides or even to the front. If the backs of your hands face forward, as they should, then try holding them so that the palms are at your sides and the backs of your hands face out. Sense what happens in the shoulders and how soon maintaining this position becomes uncomfortable. Hold your hands so that the palms face out and notice that now instead of moving too far back, the shoulders must be thrown too far forward. Yet people who habitually hold themselves in these ways do not sense the strain that is chronically present in the shoulder joints. The strain is there and is taking its toll, but the sensory apparatus has become distorted and does not register the strain, so that the pain signals no longer come through. The body similarly suffers from locking the knees and countless other things we do that are more or less damaging to us. But our loss of awareness and our alienation from our bodies is so extreme that we continually injure ourselves without knowing it. When we hurt ourselves sufficiently to produce some condition that cannot be ignored, *then* we call it a disease or else explain it away as a symptom of aging.

It is sometimes possible to discover what the body feels but can no longer communicate to the mind by exaggerating certain visible tendencies. For instance, if the left arm habitually hangs lower than the right and pulls down the left shoulder, then if you lower the arm even further, you will feel pain that is ordinarily blocked.

Whether or not your left shoulder is lower than the right, let the left arm and shoulder sink to the left. You should then sense that this pushes up the right shoulder and also thrusts out the hip on the right side. Your weight shifts to the left foot. The spine bends to the left, compressing the rib cage on that side and expanding it on the right side. If you look in a mirror you will see that the neck is longer on the left side, whether that is your normal state or one which you are now assuming. Your breathing is somewhat impaired on that side and your freedom of movement will also be affected.

Once again observe how your arms hang as you stand normally and try to determine whether one hand is hanging lower than the other. If, as is the case with many, many people, one hand does hang lower than the other, then ask yourself whether this is something that you knew already or whether you are learning it now for the first time. If possible, stand in front of a mirror, preferably without clothing, and observe your body. Some people cannot see their own distortions even in the mirror, although they are quite obvious to others. Often the body must be photographed against a grid before the facts can be consciously accepted.

Extend your arms out in front of you at shoulder height. If your hands are also extended, let them dangle at the wrists instead. Extending the hands serves no purpose and such extension will not occur unintentionally in a well-organized body. Try to sense which hand and arm feels heavier. With almost everyone, accurate sensing will disclose that one hand and arm feels heavier. Now ask yourself which of your wrists is more flexible. Flex and extend the wrists and find out whether your impression was in fact correct. If your sensing is accurate, you will discover that the wrist of the arm that feels heavier is less flexible. The comparatively greater tension in that arm stiffens the wrist and produces the sensation of heaviness.

Put your arms down at your sides for a moment and then raise them in front of you again, letting the hands dangle without extending the wrists. Sense the weight of the hands as they dangle. Extend the hands and compare the sensation of weight with what you just felt. Make the hands into fists and compare the weight again. Sense the weight of the hands and arms with the fists clenched, with the hands extended, and with the hands dangling and the wrists limp. The arms should feel lightest when the hands are dangling, heavier when the hands are extended, and still heavier when the fists are clenched. In other words, the more tension you create in the arms, the heavier they feel. Repeat this a few times and try to sense the difference clearly. If you cannot right now, then you will be able to later, when your awareness has increased.

Now we will further explore the defects in the body image and the distortions of the kinesthetic sense. Many of the "tests" included are those given at the start of the Feldenkrais Awareness Through Movement program.

Lie on your back with your hands at your sides near your hips and simply pay attention to your body for a while. Scan its surface, notice how it lies, and whatever else may come to your attention. Close your eyes and try to sense how much of the surface of your body is actually present in your awareness. Note whether some parts are quite clear while others are more faint and see if you can also identify those parts of your body of which awareness is minimal or nonexistent. In time you will sense the surface of your body much more clearly than you do now and you will also sense your skeleton and the skeletal joints. Most people assume that they do sense the surface of their bodies and that all parts of the surface are sensed with about the same clarity. However, very few ever test the assumption.

Now sense your body's contact with the floor. Does the entire body lie flat against the floor, or do some parts make contact while other parts are raised? Some parts will never touch the floor, and many other parts should touch but do not because of excess tension in the muscles. Try to sense how much space there is between the floor and the small of your back or the lumbar spine area. Then, with your hand, explore that space and see whether it is as you sensed it to be. If you can slide your hand between the floor and the small of your back, then the spine is being held in a curved position by excessive muscular contractions. When they are relaxed, that part of the spine will lie flat. Try to sense how much space there is between the floor and the back of your neck. How many fingers do you think you could fit into that space (with the fingers on their sides, of course)? Now measure the space with your fingers and determine whether it is as you sensed it to be.

Try to sense whether there is space between the floor and the backs of your knees. Sit up a moment and, with your eyes closed, again sense the space beneath the knees. Then use your hands to find out what it is. Lie back again, and try to sense whether there is space between your wrists and the floor. Do your shoulders lie flat on the floor and if not, how far up are they raised? Press the shoulders against the floor and observe what happens with your wrists. Then flatten the wrists against the floor and see whether that causes the shoulders to move upward.

Take a little rest and, as you do so, observe your breathing and also how your body lies. Is it the same as it was when you lay down, or does anything feel different?

Continue to lie on your back with your eyes closed

and try now to sense the height of your forehead. Your arms should be resting at your sides with the palms down. Do not try to use your intellect to calculate the height of your forehead, and do not guess, but try to *sense* it. Then, with your right arm and hand extended, raise the right hand to indicate what you sense the height of the forehead to be. Open your eyes, look at the height of the hand, and compare it with the height of the forehead. Put the hand and arm back down. Close your eyes and sense the forehead once again. This time, bending your right arm at the elbow, raise the hand and forearm to indicate with the hand what you now sense the forehead's height to be. Open your eyes and compare the height of the hand with the height of the forehead. Is your hand at the same level as the first time? If not, what does it mean? Did you sense the forehead differently on the two occasions? Or do you sense the height of your hand differently depending on whether the arm is bent or extended? Why should there be any difficulty about sensing the height of the forehead and about indicating what you have sensed with your hand?

When this test is given to a group of people, the majority will raise the hand to a height much higher than that of the forehead, sometimes two or three times higher. Some will raise the hand much higher than that. Still others will elevate the hand only two or three inches off the ground. And typically there will be a considerable difference between the height indicated when the whole arm is raised and when it is bent, with only the forearm raised.

If we take these results at face value, then apparently

most people sense the head as being much larger than it actually is, while some others sense it as being very tiny, the size of a large orange or a grapefruit. What are the implications for movement, for the burden placed on the muscles to support such a head? Most people see the reflected images of their own heads a great many times daily. How can the distortion be so great between the sensing and the reality? We might add that these same extreme sensory distortions will be manifested even when a group is composed of athletes, dancers, actors, and others who might be expected to have a much better than average awareness of their bodies and their movements.

To our knowledge, no one has tried to study the effects of this particular phenomenon on behavior and use, but it would be worth doing. The human head, in any case, is heavy, weighing between twenty and twenty-five pounds in most cases. We are not ordinarily aware of this great weight, or of the muscular effort that has to be made to support it when we are standing or sitting. In fact, many people sense the interior of the head as empty space. However, a head that is sensed as much larger than it actually is will surely contribute somewhat to awkwardness of movement and to the excessive muscular tensions so commonly found in the neck and the upper back and shoulders.

Again with your eyes closed, try to sense as clearly as possible the distance between the corners of your mouth. Then with your two index fingers indicate what you sense the width of your mouth to be. Open your eyes and compare the distance between your fingers with the actual width of your mouth. The distortion is typically less here than it is when most other parts of the body are sensed, but it still may be considerable. The lips and the mouth are sensed better than most other parts of the body because they are so frequently used—for eating, speaking, kissing. They are also, of course, very richly equipped for sensing.

Once again lie with your arms at your sides, palms down, and this time sense the width of your head, again relying just on your senses and not on memory or mental calculations. Now with your hands indicate what you sense the width of your head to be. Open your eyes and compare the distance between your hands with the actual width of your head. In this case the distortion will typically be greater than when you sensed the width of your mouth, but less than when the effort was made to sense the height of your forehead. As you consider these matters, note whether you are breathing freely or whether you tend to hold your breath. Try to remember whether you held your breath when sensing the width of your head, and think about whether you typically hold your breath whenever you are in novel situations or attempting to solve some problem.

Get up and move around the room for a while, noticing how you move when you walk. Note how much you bend your knees and your elbows and how each arm moves in relation to the leg that goes forward as you walk. Continuing to observe, think about whether this is the normal relationship of your arm and leg movements or whether your self-observation is altering your behavior. Remember what you observed the first time you did this and compare that to what you observed this time.

Then lie down once again. Close your eyes and sense your body. See whether it lies any differently now, whether the back lies any flatter than before and whether any other changes may have occurred simply because you have been paying an unaccustomed amount of attention to your body.

Focus your attention on your feet. How much do your feet and toes incline away from your body, if at all? Is the angle the same on both sides, or does the outside of one foot come closer to the floor? Do you feel that your legs are also tilted out to the sides because of something that is happening in the hip joints? As you bring the outside of one foot closer to the floor, note the sensation and the movement in the hip joint. Some people will point their toes straight up, without tilting their feet outward. They are not conscious of the effort required to maintain the legs in that strained position. Hold your feet so that the toes point up—*without* holding your breath. Keep them in that position for a while and compare what you are feeling now with what you feel when you allow your legs to lie normally.

Close your eyes and try to sense the shape and the weight of your eyeballs. Then, keeping your eyes closed, look back and forth from left to right a number of times. Do it as if you were watching a Ping-Pong ball bouncing back and forth on a table that keeps getting longer and longer. Try a tennis match for a while. Note whether you move your mouth as you look from left to right, and whether your breathing is normal. Stop for a moment and see whether you can now sense the outline and weight of your eyeballs more clearly.

Some of these simple tests should have convinced you of both the need for greater awareness and the real possibility of increasing your bodily awareness and learning more about yourself. Before concluding this chapter, we will try to show how quickly and easily the muscle system and movement in general can be improved if the brain is addressed directly. The changes will probably not be permanent or very extensive, but in time they can be.

Now stand up and make sure not to move your feet throughout this short sequence of movements. Only then will you be able to feel and measure what you have accomplished.

Place your hands on your hips and twist your body as far as you can to the right without straining, and stay in that position for a moment. Note how far you have turned by marking the position on the wall with your eyes. Now, as you move your eyes farther to the right, notice that the muscles will relax so that you will be able to look somewhat farther to the right than you could just a moment ago. Now turn your body back toward the left and stop in a position facing forward, as you were at the beginning.

Next extend both your arms out to the sides at shoulder height. Once again twist as far you can can to the right, allowing your eyes to move freely to the right as you turn. Look once again at the wall and you should see that you now have turned somewhat farther than you could just a moment ago. Turn left and come back to your original position. Put your hands on your hips as you did for the first movement. Now twist your body to the right once again, eyes also to the right, and you should find that you can turn at least as far as you did with the arms extended, and considerably farther than you could just moments ago with your hands on the hips as you now have them.

How much flexibility have you gained with just these very few movements in such a short time? A few more simple movements would substantially increase the flexibility. The improvement you experienced could only occur because the muscles released some of their tension, giving greater freedom to the spine. The conventional approach to increasing freedom of movement is to gradually stretch the muscles so as to lengthen them. Obviously in so brief a time and with so few movements the muscles were not stretched to produce the changes you experienced. Rather, the brain stopped contracting the muscles, so that they could lengthen instantly.

Now just one more demonstration (which requires bare feet):

Walk around a little and compare the movement in the legs. Note how the right foot makes contact with the floor, then the left one. Stand still and notice how you are standing. Then position yourself next to a wall or some object you can use to help balance and support yourself for a few minutes. Place your right hand against the wall, or take hold of the object for support.

Slide your left foot along the floor, forward and

backward, trying to sense the floor with the entire bottom of the foot, or as much as you can. Do this and each of the movements at least fifteen times, twenty-five would be better. Stop and rest whenever you need to.

Now slide just the toes of the left foot forward and backward as before. Do the same with the toes and the ball of the foot. Then with the heel only, up to twenty-five times.

Stop for a moment. Now move the tips of your toes forward and backward. After that, make circles on the floor with the tips of your toes, first clockwise, then counterclockwise.

Make circles on the floor with your heel. Clockwise for a while, then counterclockwise. Then do the same thing with the whole bottom of the foot.

Turn your left foot onto its outer edge, or as far as you can easily go in that direction. Slide the foot forward and backward on its outer edge. Then turn the foot toward the instep and slide it forward and backward.

Slide the entire bottom of the foot forward and backward again, paying attention to what you are sensing. Note the sensation in the heel, along the sole of the foot, the ball of the foot, the toes. See what you can learn about the floor by sensing with your foot. Then pay attention to the sensations in the foot. And stop.

Now think about the way you are standing. Does the left foot make better contact with the floor, indicating release of muscle tension? Walk around a little and observe how you walk—the way the left foot falls, and the right, the movement in the knees and the hip joints. Do you walk more lightly on the left side? Do your eyes tend to look a little to the left?

Lie down on the floor and sense your body. See whether the left side feels longer, and whether it lies more completely on the floor than does the right side. Close your eyes to sense it, and try to determine whether the left side really is longer. Open your eyes and see whether you look somewhat to the left. The eyes will always tend to look over to the side where some improvement has been achieved. Try to observe whether the left side of your body is more clearly in your awareness—a better body image.

These two examples provide but the barest hints of what you can achieve. Your body can change with ease and rapidity, and that is just as true of the elderly as it is of other age groups. Nor should your present physical condition, if it is short of catastrophic, interfere with your improvement.

How to Do the Exercises

MOST OF THE REMAINDER of this book will consist of exercises selected to illustrate the varieties of experience and change Psychophysical Reeducation makes possible. We cannot, in a book, cover all the possibilities, but we can give you enough so that you can make many quite remarkable gains in your use and your functioning. Doing even one exercise on a single occasion will be beneficial. But if you continue the work for a year, practicing the exercises several times a week or more, you will be able to reeducate yourself to a remarkable extent, with benefits greater than you would be likely to believe if we enumerated them for you now. There will always be room for improvement, even if you work to the end of your life—an end which should come later, rather than sooner, with this work. Your true potential is rich enough to continue to unfold for a lifetime.

Now, we will tell you first of all how to arrange matters so that your practice of the exercises will be made as easy as possible. In doing so, we would rather say the obvious than omit some point you need to know and might not think about. First, try to have a comfortable space in which to do the work. You should have ample room on the floor so that you can extend your arms out to your sides without being distracted by the possibility of bumping into some object. In general, any diversion of your attention away from the exercises will diminish the results which otherwise would be obtained. Therefore, take whatever measures are needed to insure that your exercise period will not be interrupted. If you have a telephone, unplug it, muffle it, do whatever is required to prevent the device from obstructing your work. Similarly, do not try to do the exercises if you are expecting someone to arrive or if other interruptions are likely. The situation is not at all the same as it would be were you doing conventional exercise. Doing mindless repetitions of movements is one thing; focusing attention to cultivate refined awareness is quite another.

It is, of course, desirable to have a pleasant room to work in, and when the weather is suitable, the windows should be opened—unless they let in distracting noises as well as fresh air. As a general rule, it is not a good practice to do any kind of exercise in a draft.

It is best to do the exercises nude or wearing as little

clothing as possible. If you must wear something, be sure it is loose and does not obstruct your movements. You should not be aware of the clothing as you work.

You should be as comfortable as possible in all respects. This means that you should have a rug or a mat that is pleasant to work on. Do not allow yourself to be distracted by trying to work on an uncomfortable surface. Discomfort not only diminishes the results, it undermines your motivation to do regular work. It is possible to do most of the exercises on a bed, should that be necessary.

In every aspect of the work there should be an emphasis on making it just as pleasurable as possible. It is well known that ordinary physical training is not usually a pleasurable experience. Many students try to avoid it, and most people tend to discontinue systematic exercise as soon as it is no longer compulsory—and to resume it only when the body's deterioration or some illness makes it a necessity. Any discomfort, any strain, any competition or insistence on goals to be achieved, will always constitute a form of negative conditioning. It is this negative conditioning which erodes motivation, demanding a countereffort by the will, which is itself unpleasant and obstructive.

Feldenkrais has insisted upon the development of a teaching method that reinforces motivation by means of positive conditioning rather than undermining it through the usual negative conditioning. He has observed that people learn best when the learning is pleasant and that such learning is also better retained. Education that is pleasurable and that provides contin-

uous objective proofs of significant improvement
should be possible in most areas of learning. In the
case of exercise, many people must first of all free
themselves from the notion that the harder they work,
the better the results. In fact, as these exercises will
demonstrate, exactly the opposite is true. The harder
you try to improve a movement, for example, the less
the movement will improve. When the element of striv-
ing has been eliminated, improvement will come easily
and often exceed all expectations. The usual approach
is to try to force your body, thereby introducing tension and strain, and generating internal conflict, so that
the body naturally tends to resist. The more effective
way is to utilize pleasurable movements to indicate to
the brain and nervous system what is desired. When
this is done, the brain will organize the body to yield almost effortlessly results far better than those which
could be achieved by the usual boring, if not self-tor-
turing, methods. As these experiences of better functioning are repeated, the distortions of the kinesthetic
sense will be corrected. Fortunately, the nervous system is basically hedonistic and will always prefer the
optimal, more pleasurable way of functioning when
given the choice.

To avoid strain and negative conditioning, always do
only what is well within your present capabilities. Not
only should any movement be stopped short of the
point where it is painful or has to be forced, but no
movements should be continued long enough to become fatiguing or in any other way stressful. If you
feel tired, stop, rest a bit, and then continue. You will

learn that when you rest from the physical movements, you can effectively continue the exercise by imagining the movements and accompanying sensations. These imaginary actions will often yield an even greater improvement than you obtained from the physical ones. Rest periods will also be utilized for the purpose of scanning the body and observing the changes the movements have produced.

At the end of a session, because all strain has been avoided, you should not feel tired. In fact, you should feel more relaxed and have more energy after forty-five minutes of a psychophysical exercise than at the beginning.

As you practice the exercises, your attention will repeatedly be drawn to the fact that much more is involved in your movements than you ordinarily recognize. You will learn that in making almost any movement, far more of your movements are unconscious than are conscious. For instance, when making a particular leg movement, a person typically remains quite unaware of what he is doing at the same time with many other parts of his body—his shoulders, his rib cage, parts involved in breathing, his mouth, his eyes, the foot of the other leg, and so on. All these parts are visibly involved in his movement, and yet he is so intent on moving the leg that he banishes most of the rest of his body from consciousness. When what was banished is restored, it may become apparent that some of the other parts have been working in opposition to the movement of the leg. So divided is the body within itself, and so much in conflict can the mind and

body be, that even in very gross ways we thwart ourselves and create the conditions for our failures and
our piecemeal self-destruction. As more of the body is
brought into awareness, with the formerly unconscious
movements made conscious, it becomes possible for the
first time to live in a more integrated and effective way.

The typical exercise lasts about forty-five minutes,
and you will be expected to focus your attention exclu-
sively on your body for the whole of that time. To most
people this may sound like an impossible, or at least
very difficult, task, calling for an effort of concentration that demands a great exertion of the will. However, this prolonged attention, like the movements,
should be easy and free of strain if it is to be effective.
Therefore, the exercises have been structured so as to
facilitate the sustained attention, making it, too, effortless. This can be achieved by what we have termed
the *seduction of consciousness by novelty*—the use of new
experiences which are pleasurable and unusual enough
to maintain the focus of consciousness on the body.

Such experiences are provided continuously through
each exercise. Because the movements are pleasurable,
or at least not unpleasurable, consciousness does not
seek to escape as it would from something that was unpleasant. Furthermore, the many novel and unfamiliar
movements we have provided will help to sustain your
interest in whatever is actually occurring and your curi-
osity about whatever is going to happen next.

Clearly recognizable changes in the body's condition—for instance, in sensations of length and weight,
in the clarity of different parts of the body image, in

the freedom of the joints, and in the increasing ease and fluidity of the movements being made—will repeatedly be called to your attention as you experience them, since otherwise, most would go unnoticed, extreme as some of the changes are. This and other aspects of the work will tend to keep your consciousness focused on your body and prolong your attention in a way that otherwise would probably require prodigious effort on your part. Later you will find that your powers of concentration have been enhanced by the prolonged attention paid in the course of the exercises.

In general, all movements should be easy and light, and they should be done rather slowly unless otherwise indicated. When the text calls for quick movements, increase the speed but be sure that you do not sacrifice your awareness. When you emphasize the quality of both movement and awareness, then you will be able to move quickly without rushing or otherwise acting in compulsive ways.

As you observe your own way of doing various movements, you will probably become aware of tendencies in yourself which determine not only how you move, but your approach to life in general. Compulsive people will find themselves wanting to do the movements in ways which are clearly compulsive. Some will discover that they habitually use much more force, and so expend much more energy, than an action calls for. Others will note that it is very difficult for them to think and act at the same time—that thinking interferes with action, while acting impairs mental effort.

Most people will discover again and again that they hold their breath when they face an unusual problem or make an unaccustomed effort. When this occurs there will also be superfluous tensions in the muscles, with some parts of the body held rigid. As you observe these tendencies in yourself you will begin to change them. Old patterns of compulsiveness and excessive use of force, for example, will begin to break up, and when this happens, physical changes will occur which will yield psychological and emotional changes as well. The exercises cannot completely overcome deep-rooted emotional problems, but they can yield quite significant gains, such as reduction of anxiety and rigidities of thinking and feeling.

Unless otherwise indicated, most of the movements in the exercises should be repeated about twenty-five times (fewer at the start if that is too many for you). This is the number of repetitions done in most basic Feldenkrais exercises, and found to be most effective in bringing about the desired amount of change in muscle tones. When twenty-five repetitions are done, the average exercise will require about forty to forty-five minutes to complete.

There are various ways of performing the exercises included in this book. One way is to read a few lines or a paragraph, then perform the movements, go back and read a few more lines, and so on. At least several exercises should be done in this way, so that you get a good sense of how long the sequences of movements and the rest periods take. When the method is familiar, then it may be easier to put the exercises on cassette audio tapes and thereafter work from the tapes. The

90- or 120-minute tapes are recommended, so that one complete exercise can be transcribed on each side of a tape. The exercises also can be done with two people, one reading from the book, the other doing the movements—an especially good way to proceed, since much can be learned from a partner. If tapes are made, they may be more effective if recorded while reading the exercises to someone else and observing the time required for movements and rest. Once the tapes have been made, then of course two or more people can exercise together.[1]

It is not likely that in the beginning you will be able to memorize the exercises from the book and so avoid either referring back to the text or making tape recordings. The exercises have too many movements, and the movements are too unfamiliar, to be readily memorized. Some may not have been done since childhood or even infancy. Later, when the movements have become familiar and awareness is sufficiently increased, it will be possible to do the exercises from memory. Until then, however, we think you will find that the effects will greatly outweigh the initial inconvenience.

Eventually, with application, you will grasp the principles underlying the exercises. Then you will be able to create new exercises to work with any part of your body or any function that you wish to improve.

Finally, the first time you do the exercises, please do

[1] Inquiries concerning taped instruction by the authors should be addressed to us at P.O. Box 600, Pomona, N.Y. 10970. Also available are taped "Awareness Through Movement" lessons by Dr. Moshe Feldenkrais, Big Sur Recordings, Big Sur, Calif. 93920, which will be of great use to the serious student.

them in the order given. There are important reasons why you should do so. Later, you can do them as you please, although you should always do a variety of them, not just a few favorites.

Part 2

Psychophysical Exercises

Improving Head, Neck, and Eye Movements

ACCORDING TO ALEXANDER, misuse of the body most often begins in that region where the neck joins the torso; and for other reasons as well, he regarded this region as the most important "use area." When the condition of this part of the body is improved, it becomes easier to bring about improvement in the other parts.

> This whole region at the base of the neck, both back and front, is a veritable maelstrom of muscular coordination. It is here that those most inadequate evolutionary adaptations—the shoulders and upper arms—will exert their distorting influence during the many activities in which we engage. It is here that faulty patterns of breathing

throw the muscles of the lower neck and upper ribs into excessive spasm; it is here that mechanisms of speech and swallowing require a reasonably good vertebral posture if the oesophagus and trachea and associated vocal structures are to function well. It is close to here that blood vessels and nerves of great importance and complexity will pass—blood vessels to the base of the brain, nerve ganglia which affect breathing and heart rate and blood pressure, nerve roots which with increasing age become more and more liable to compression: it is here that 85% of the readers of this book will have arthritis by the time they are 55 (and many of them much younger than that): and it is from here that the head itself—the structure which carries man's most important sensory equipment of sight and hearing, taste and smell, and balance—has to be coordinated at rest and in movement . . . it is here that we have to start if we are to correct the multitudinous mis-uses which the rest of the body can throw up.[1]

The first two psychophysical exercises will work in this primary area. In the first exercise, we will eliminate some of the muscular tensions in the neck and back, allowing the head to turn more freely. We will also release some of the tension in the eye muscles and better coordinate the movement of the eyes with the head and neck movements. Some eye movements which, for most readers, will have hitherto been unconscious, will be made conscious. The reader will begin to be aware of, and learn to apply, effective body mechanics.

[1] Barlow, *The Alexander Principle*, p. 28.

To begin, lie on your back. Close your eyes and observe how your body is lying. Pay particular attention to your spine, your back, and your shoulders. How much space is there between the small of your back and the floor? Between the back of your neck and the floor? Use your hand and your fingers to determine if these spaces are as you sensed them to be. Is the space under the neck the same if you measure it on the left side as it is when you measure it on the right side? Is there a difference between the left shoulder's contact with the floor and that of the right shoulder? Compare the left buttock with the right. Are there spaces between your wrists and the floor, and are the spaces the same or different for the two wrists? How about the right knee and the left? The calves? Do your two hands lie the same? And is your breathing symmetrical? That is, do you breathe with equal freedom through both nostrils? As you breathe, do your lungs expand equally on both sides? Do you feel the breathing, or the effects of the breathing, in your shoulders? in your back?

Pay attention to the way the head is lying. Note whether your nose points straight up and whether, when your eyes are open, your eyes look straight up. If the eyes look a little to one side, then is the head tilted slightly, so that the nose points to one side?

Now close your eyes. Turn your head to the left and then to the right, however far it will go without forcing or straining. Keep turning the head from one side to the other and observe whether it turns more easily, and goes farther, to one side than to the other. If it turns better to one side than to the other, consider whether that fact is related to what you observed about the shoulders, the back, etc. When you have turned the head from left to right at least twenty-five times, take a rest.

At all times, unless otherwise instructed, please lie with your arms down at your sides, the hands resting palms down, somewhere near the thighs and buttocks. Now, push your hands down toward your feet a little, bring them back to where they were, push down again, and continue to do that. This means that the shoulders and arms also move down. Combine that movement with the turning of the head from side to side. When you turn your head left, the left hand should slide down in the direction of your feet. When you turn your head right, the right hand should slide down. This should mean that when you turn your head to the left, the left shoulder goes down and the right one comes up; and when you turn your head right, the right shoulder goes down and the left one comes up. Turn the head left to right until it seems natural for the shoulders to move up and down as the head moves. Then stop and rest a little while. After that, turn your head a few times from left to right.

Now put your two hands together on your body, somewhere below your navel, letting one rest on top of the other. Continue turning your head left to right, allowing it to turn as far as it will go without discomfort. Your upper body can roll a little as you do that. When the head goes left, the right shoulder and part of the back on the right side can leave the floor a little. When the head goes right, the left shoulder and part of the back can leave the floor. However, keep the movement in your upper body as much as possible. Remember to do fifteen to twenty-five repetitions, or more.

Fold your arms across your chest and see whether it becomes still easier to turn your head from left to right, and whether the movement becomes still more extensive. Then stop for a moment.

Put your arms down at your sides with the palms of your hands down. And just *imagine* turning your head from left to right. Imagine it vividly, what it feels like, how far the head goes to each side, and how quickly you do it. Imagine that you fold your arms over your chest and continue to imagine turning the head. Imagine that at least ten times, taking care that you breathe freely as you do it. When you imagined the movement with the arms folded over the chest, did you imagine that the shoulders and the back left the floor?

Now do a few more imaginary movements, and notice whether, as you imagine turning left, your eyes look to the left, and when you imagine turning right, your eyes turn to the right. See if you can imagine turning the head and shoulders to the left and the right *without* moving your eyes. Imagine the sensations and the movement while deliberately immobilizing your eyes, which should be looking straight ahead. Note whether your breathing remains free. Now imagine letting your eyes move freely along with the imagined movements of the head.

Now, with your hands still lying at your sides, the palms down, imagine turning your head and that when your head turns left, the left shoulder goes down and the right shoulder comes up—the same movements you did earlier. When your head goes right, the right shoulder goes down and the left shoulder comes up. Down is, of course, toward your feet, and up is toward your head. The reference is to your body as it would be in a standing position. As we will see, your body understands that *it* determines up and down, not the space in which you lie, although your mind may think of up and down in terms of the ceiling and the floor. Continue to imagine turning your head, the shoulders moving up and down. Now, with your eyes open, actually turn your head quickly from side to side. Notice whether your shoulders go up and down as the head turns, and do so spontaneously. Then stop, rest, and close your eyes.

Imagine that you are standing in a meadow and looking at a small growing plant with a most interesting flower. Now imagine that you are looking at a great majestic tree towering upward into the sky and clouds. Then imagine that you are looking at the waters of a lake, observing the reflection of the clouds, or your own reflection, in the waters. And next imagine that you are looking at a mountain peak covered with snow. Once again, with your eyes closed, imagine that you are looking at the plant with its interesting flower. Open your eyes and observe where you are looking. Close your eyes and again imagine looking at the tree, its majestic branches raised against the sky. Open your eyes and see where you are looking. Close them, and imagine looking at the surface of the lake, at the reflections in the water. Open your eyes and see where you are looking. Close your eyes and imagine looking at the snow-capped mountain peak. Open your eyes and see where you are looking. Now almost everyone should understand what we meant when we said that the body establishes up and down in terms of itself. Down is toward the feet and up is toward the head, and when you imagine a scene, your eyes move as they would if you were looking at space outside of yourself. However, few people are conscious of the movements of the eyes which occur when they fantasize or imagine, just as few people are conscious of changes in the muscles, breathing, etc., when action is imaginary. In the case of the eye movements, that hitherto unconscious movement has just been brought into awareness.

Now close your eyes once again. Imagine looking at the flower and be aware of your eyes looking down. Imagine looking at the tree and sense your eyes looking up. Imagine looking at the lake, at the mountain-top, and note again the movement of the eyes. Imagine looking at something far over to your left, and then at something far over to your right. Imagine something far over to your right, open your eyes and see where you are looking. Do the same thing on the left side.

Now close your eyes. Put your arms over your chest. *Imagine* turning your head from left to right, so that the shoulders follow the movement of the head and neck. Do it once or twice actually, physically, so that you get a good sense of it: Turn your head left, letting the right shoulder and back come off the floor. Turn your head right so that the left shoulder and back are involved in that movement. Then imagine those movements, and as you do them be aware of your eyes going left when your head goes left, and right when your head goes right. Although the head movement is imaginary, imagining it may cause a very slight actual movement of the head even though you do not intend it. There will be a change in the muscles and at least a minuscle movement whether you are aware of them or not.

Again, imagine turning your head and see if you sense any change in the muscles, or a slight tendency to move. The eyes should be allowed to move freely. Then see how clearly you can imagine the movement while keeping the eyes immobile. Then imagine letting the eyes move very freely. Actually turn your head left and right, eyes closed but looking far over to the left as you turn left, and far over to the right as you turn right.

Now open your eyes and repeat the movement. The arms should be folded across the chest. Turn, looking far to the left as you go left, looking far to the right as you go right. Put your hands down at your sides, palms down, and turn your head left to right, letting the shoulders and hands go up and down on the floor, as you have done before. Be sure that the eyes look left as the head turns left, and right as the head turns right. Then stop and rest for a while.

Now look left with your *closed* eyes and imagine the head and neck turning left. Look right with the closed eyes and imagine the head and the neck turning right. Do that a number of times. Now we will do it a different way. This time look right with your eyes as you imagine the head and neck turning left, and imagine your head turning right as the eyes look to the left. Breathe freely and continue to repeat the movements. Then actually turn your head and neck right and left while opposing the eye movements to those of the head. After a while, let the head and the eyes go together—both to the right, both to the left—and let the shoulders do whatever they will.

Now open your eyes and turn your head from side to side. Put your arms across your chest and do it, head and eyes to the right, head and eyes to the left.

Finally, put your arms down at your sides once again. Turn your head from left to right, noticing how it rolls now and comparing that movement with the way it was at the start of the exercise. Note whether your eyes now spontaneously go well over to the left and to the right as the head turns, the eyes not looking straight ahead but very definitely looking to the left when the head goes left, and to the right when the head goes right. When the head has gone as far right as it will go, see whether, although your head faces the wall, your eyes are looking down toward the floor. It should be just the same when you turn left, making plain to you that the eyes are turning along with the head. This movement of the eyes allows the head to turn farther than it otherwise would, by releasing muscles in the neck.

Lie quietly and scan your body, letting your consciousness roam over its parts. Sense how the neck is lying, the back, the lower spine, the buttocks, the legs,

the arms. Note whether there is any difference between the body's contact with the floor now and the
way it was when you observed it at the beginning. Roll
slowly to one side and get up. As you move around,
sense whether your body seems somewhat more erect,
perhaps a little taller. Walk around and, when you
turn, pay attention to what your eyes do. Observe
whether your eyes are active participants in that turning. See if you can sense the instant when you begin to
turn and whether your eyes turn in that direction also.
Try to determine what part of the body turns *first,* and
the sequences of movements in the various parts of
your body as you turn. Do you turn first at the hip
joint, or do your eyes turn first? Try to figure it out
while walking, and also while standing still. You may
find it is not so easy to determine what moves first,
much less the entire sequence of movements involved
in turning, even when you stand still.

Increasing Mobility of the Shoulders

THIS SECOND PSYCHOPHYSICAL EXERCISE will also improve the situation in the primary area of misuse. By markedly reducing the excess tensions in the muscles of the back, it will enable the shoulder joints to move with an unusual degree of freedom, and that freedom will also allow the head and neck to move better.

What is meant by the shoulders will be found to vary considerably from one person to the next. One, when he thinks of the shoulder or shoulders, is thinking mainly of the joints. Another thinks mainly of the upper portion of the arms, while a third might think of the shoulders primarily in terms of the shoulder blades and back.

The way that the shoulders are held will allow or inhibit free movement of the neck. For example, simply turn your head from side to side, observing the movement of your head and neck as you do so. Then draw your shoulders back in a kind of military posture and observe how the head and neck movements are at once obstructed. If you observe more closely, you will also become aware that your breathing is impaired. To make the observation easier, exaggerate the throwing back of the shoulders, which makes the impairment more extreme. The shoulders are usually carried too high, inhibiting free movement in the joints and producing other problems as well.

We have discussed already some of the reasons why the potential for movement is lost as people grow older—much less a symptom of aging than of misuse—and how some of this potential diminishes even during childhood. Here we will mention a rather curious finding that emerged from a series of experiments with hypnotic age regression.

During these experiments, people were regressed to earlier and earlier ages and, at different ages, were encouraged to explore as completely as possible the body's sensations and its ability to move. The person would be regressed as far back as possible and then brought forward in time to his current age. During both the regression and the progression, changes in bodily functioning were noted. The most striking discovery was that many women, when regressed back to childhood, experienced great mobility in the shoulder joints and in the body generally, but at about the time of puberty, reported a very definite loss of shoulder mobility. The way in which the shoulders were held changed, and the entire body became more rigid. Tension was introduced into the back and the neck, and, during the course of the experiments at least, this tension did not thereafter dissipate, nor was the movement of the shoulders or the arms ever again as free. Some of the subjects related this change to menstruation and others to the awakening of sexual feelings which they evidently had tried to suppress. In any case, the response to puberty was a tightening of the upper part of the body, especially around the shoulders. This change was much more pronounced than any reported in the pelvic region or in any other part of the lower body.

These experiments also showed that other major changes in the life of the subject had produced marked changes in the state of the musculature and, in some instances, of the skeletal alignment. This occurred when a significant event had aroused strong ambivalence or negative feelings. Abuse by a parent or someone else, the parents' divorce, death in the immediate family, serious problems at school, had introduced muscular tensions, inhibited movement, including breathing, and led to the adoption of other abnormal use patterns. Some subjects believed that these bodily changes were accompanied by a significant decrease in self-esteem, increases in anxiety or emotional rigidity, and thinking and learning difficulties. Whatever one's opinion of hypnotic age regression, the subjects' observations (or inventions) are essentially correct, and changes of these kinds should be recognized and dealt with when they occur, as they very rarely are.

To begin with, take a standing position. Raise your arms to shoulder height in front of you, then lower and raise them repeatedly. Raise them overhead and lower them, noting the feelings in the shoulders as you move.

Let your arms hang at your sides and raise your shoulders up and down several times. Then rotate the shoulders in a forward direction a few times. Also rotate them backward a few times, always noting the quality of the movement as well as the sensations.

Let your arms hang at your sides, then swing them forward and back. Make circles with your hands and arms, circling in one direction for a while, and then in the opposite direction, again noting what it feels like in your shoulders.

Lie down on your back and let your consciousness roam over the surface of your body. Note especially how your shoulders lie, and whether they are in contact with the floor. If they are not, how high are they raised off the floor? Can you identify any of the muscular tension that prevents them from sinking down? Observe how your hands and arms lie. How far away from your body are your hands? Are your palms facing down or up? If your palms are down, note whether your wrists lie flat or whether they are bent somewhat, so that there is a space between the wrists and the floor. Compare the two wrists, and also the hands, the arms, and the shoulders.

Observe how your back lies on the floor. If the muscles are properly relaxed, then almost the entire surface of the back will make good contact with the floor. If only certain parts of your back are touching, then there is too much tension. How much space do you sense beneath your lumbar spine (the small of the back)? Use your hand to determine whether it is about as you sensed it. Does the spine lie as it did the last time you checked it?

Now scan the front of your body. Do you feel that you are lying symmetrically, or do you feel that some of the parts of your body go off at curious angles? Try to arrange yourself so that you are perfectly symmetrical. For many people this will prove to be a formidable task.

Now cross your arms over your chest and take hold of your two elbows with your hands (or as close as you can come to it). Raise your arms in front of you and then move them from side to side, so that the left elbow approaches the floor on the left side and then the right elbow approaches the floor on the right side. Whether you touch the floor with the elbow is unimportant, but keep going from side to side until you have done the customary twenty-five movements, or fewer if necessary. (Figure 1.)

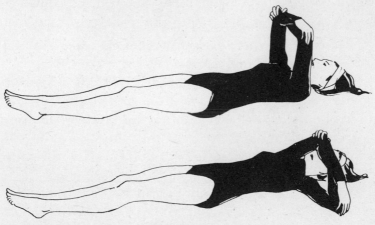

Figure 1

Now continue that movement, letting your head go along with the elbows. Your head should go left when the left elbow goes left and right when the right elbow goes right. Do the usual number of movements and then take a rest. Stop

Take hold of your elbows with your hands again and move them from left to right, letting the head go with the arms. Continue moving your elbows from side to side, but reverse the movement of the head. When the arms go right, let the head go left; when the arms go left, the head goes right. It is just the same movement as before, except that the head now opposes the movement of the arms. Rest for a few moments. - 25

Now do a sequence moving the arms from side to side *without* moving the head. You can keep your head from moving by fixing your gaze on some point on the ceiling.

Stop a moment. Do the movement once more and again let the head and arms go together. Head and arms to the left, then head and arms to the right. Try it with your eyes closed and also with your eyes open, and observe whether that affects the movement. At the end of the series, rest briefly.

While resting, always put your arms down at your sides so that you will be able to make comparisons between how you were lying before and how you lie presently. By always returning to the same position you can better note any changes in your body and in the body image.

Now raise your arms above you toward the ceiling and clasp your hands. Bring your arms over to the left and as they go over let your left wrist bend. Otherwise,

keep both of your arms perfectly straight. With your
left wrist bent, go on over to touch the floor with your
left arm, or however close you can come to the floor
without straining. Remember: it is the quality of the
movement and the quality of your attention that matter, not how close you can come to the floor. Repeat
the movement as usual. (Figure 2.) 25

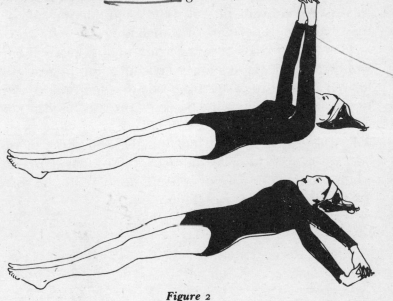

Figure 2

Keep your arms together and hands clasped, but
now move them to the right, bending just the right
wrist. Apart from that, the arms should remain
straight. Approach the floor with the right arm and
wrist. Do a number of these movements.

Then keep going from side to side, left to right,
bending the left wrist and then the right wrist in order
to facilitate the movement. As much as possible, keep

the movement in your shoulders. Nothing will be gained if you roll the entire body from side to side. See how far to the side you can go without raising either buttock from the floor. 25

Try to touch the floor *without* bending either wrist, keeping the two hands clasped and the arms and wrists straight. This time allow your body to roll a little more to assist the movement, but try to keep that movement mostly in the upper part of your body. 25

Then, instead of clasping your hands, place them with palms and fingers together, hands and fingers extended. Move your arms from side to side again, trying to touch on the left with the left arm and hand, then on the right with the right arm and hand. The head will have to move from left to right with the arms if you are to get closer to the floor. Note what happens when you fix your gaze on a point on the ceiling so that the head does not move. (Figure 3.) 25

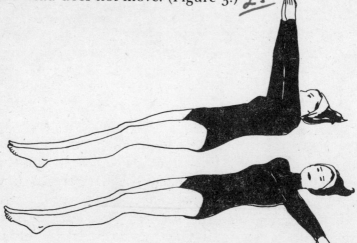

Figure 3

Do the same movement with the arms but look to the left when your arms go right, and look to the right when your arms go left. Observe how difficult it becomes, how greatly this restricts the movement. *few*

Now if you let your head and upper body go with the movement, you will move much more easily from side to side, coming a good deal closer to the floor or actually touching the floor.- *few*

Remember to breathe freely as you move, and observe what your heels, pelvis, and the sides of your legs are doing. Let your feet go all the way over, so that when you bring your arms to the left, the side of the left foot touches the floor, and when you go over to the right, the side of the right foot touches. Do that a number of times and then stop and rest a while.- *25*

Raise both your arms toward the ceiling. Let the wrists bend and the hands hang limp. Using the shoulders to do it, lift your hands closer to the ceiling and then let them back down. As you continue to do this your shoulders will rap on the floor. The raps should be quick and easy. (Figure 4.) *25*

Figure 4

Alternate the movements, so that one shoulder goes up as the other one comes down. Do this for a while, and then once again rap with both shoulders together. When the sequence is completed, have another rest.

Now place your palms on your chest with your upper arms at shoulder height and your elbows on the floor at your sides. Raise the elbows toward the ceiling and bring them back to the floor, like wings flapping. Keep on flapping your wings toward the ceiling and then back to the floor. (Figure 5.)

Figure 5

Stop for a minute, letting your hands rest on your chest and your elbows rest on the floor.

Now flap them a few more times up and down, toward the ceiling and back down to the floor.

Then start making circles with your elbows. Rotate the shoulders around in a forward movement. Make some little circles with the elbows, and then somewhat larger ones, and then the biggest circles you can, but keep the movement light and easy. Alternate between the different kinds of circles. Rest a little whenever you feel like it, and while you rest imagine making circles with your elbows. Stop

Now make more actual circles with the elbows, small circles first and then some larger ones. Reverse your direction, so that you rotate the shoulders in the opposite way. Go one way for a while, and then the other way. Stop

Bring the elbows down to the floor with the hands still resting on the chest. Flap the elbows up and down once again. Then flap them a different way, so that the elbows come down and touch your ribs at the sides of your body, and then go back to shoulder height, your hands remaining on your chest.

Do some more of these movements and then rest. Observe whether your hands lie any differently. Now raise your hands and arms above you, over your head, the backs of the hands touching or approaching the floor. Bring the arms and hands back down to your sides, touching the floor. Move them back overhead so that the hands touch the floor or approach it, as before. Keep on for a while, bringing your hands down by your thighs, then over your head toward the floor.

Stop in the middle of the movement, when your hands are closest to the ceiling. Let the wrists go limp and the hands dangle. Make circles with both hands and arms, small ones and then some bigger ones. Make the biggest circles you can, which may mean that your hands will touch the floor as you circle. Reverse the movement and circle in the opposite direction. ‑Stop

Let the left arm come down to your side and make circles with just the right one. Then put the right arm down and make a number of circles with the left arm. Make circles in one direction for a while, and then in the other direction. Let any other parts of your body move to assist with the circling. Do that while making circles again with the right arm. Stop.

Lie on your back and rest. Then, with your palms on the floor at your sides, slide your hands up and down along the floor. You should use your shoulders to push and pull your hands and arms up and down. Do the same thing with your hands and arms on top of your thighs.

Raise your arms over your head, with the backs of your hands touching the floor, or as close to the floor as they will go. Use your shoulders to push and pull the arms up and down, as you did when they were at your sides.

After that, take another rest.

Now put your arms over your chest and take hold of your elbows as you did at the beginning. Move your arms from side to side again, bringing the left elbow toward the floor on the left, the right elbow toward the floor on the right. See if you now have more freedom in your shoulder joints than you had at the beginning. Do the movement quickly but easily. Make it light, quick, and nimble.

Stop, keeping your hands on your elbows. Raise your arms toward the ceiling, above your head, and then

back down to your chest. Just move up and down instead of from side to side, making it quick and easy.
Now do it from side to side again a few times. Slide
your hands down a little so that they hold your
forearms instead of your elbows. Again move the arms
from side to side.

Stop and rest. Clasp your hands and raise your arms
toward the ceiling, and move them from side to side
several times. Let the left wrist bend as you go toward
the floor on the left side, and the right wrist bend as
you go toward the floor on the right. See if you can
make the movement a quick, easy one.

Having done that a few times, put your arms at your
sides, palms down, and note how your body lies. Observe, especially, the way the shoulders lie on the floor.
Slowly roll to one side and get up.

Walk around a little, noting how your shoulders
hang and how your arms swing. Raise your arms to
shoulder height and overhead. Bring the arms down
and swing them from side to side. Observe how your
body turns from side to side, including the head and
neck movements. Walk around some more and compare the way your shoulders feel now with the way
they felt at the start of the exercise.

Enhancing Manual Dexterity

ALONG WITH THE LIPS, the hands and especially the fingers are typically the clearest parts of the body in the body image. That is because of the comparatively great use that is made of the hands, not only in manipulating objects but also in gaining information about things. So far as the tactile sense is concerned, more information is received through the hands than through any other part of the body. Parts of the hands, the fingertips in particular, are keenly sensitive.

Because of the importance of the hands in everyday life, any impairment of their movement is as distressing as it is crippling. Such impairment is nonetheless common, especially as people grow older. Stiffness, pain, and increasing clumsiness are often accepted as almost inevitable symptoms of aging. However, such symptoms are far from inevitable; in fact, in many cases, the single exercise offered in this chapter will eventually restore a high degree of flexibility to hands and wrists that have become stiff and awkward. Even long-standing pain in the joints can be relieved when this exercise is practiced frequently, along with some others.

Given the importance of manual dexterity, it is surprising that exercise programs place so little emphasis on achieving and maintaining it. Typically, their aim is to strengthen the grip, as if the hand were used mainly for crushing or as a vise. But great power in the hands—or elsewhere in the body, for that matter—is of little use to the average person. The ability to move the hands freely and with dexterity is valuable to everyone.

Although the hands are more clearly in the body image than most other parts of the body, our awareness and sensing of them is still quite imperfect. For example, the hand typically has many areas of pain which are not ordinarily sensed at all. If you apply firm fingertip pressure to the palms and backs of your hands you are likely to encounter such pain, of which you would otherwise be unconscious.

For a moment, place your hands palms down on your thighs and try to note the extent to which you are aware of one hand's entire surface. Decide whether the hand is easier to sense with the eyes closed, and whether it comes more clearly into awareness if the fingers are sensed one by one before trying to sense the whole. Compare the awareness you have of the palms of your hands as they rest upon your thighs with the awareness you have of the backs of your hands. Note whether the awareness is greater at the tips of the fingers and whether some other parts are sensed with particular clarity. Also note which parts are sensed less clearly. With your eyes closed, try to sense as precisely as possible the way the hands lie and especially the spaces between the fingers. Then open your eyes and see if your hands lie as you sensed them. Close your eyes and observe whether the hands are beginning to emerge somewhat more clearly in your awareness.

If we want to improve the dexterity of the fingers rather quickly, the best way to do so is to widen the spaces between them. When the spaces between the fingers are wider, they will move in all directions with a greater agility and ease.

How to effectively widen the spaces between the fingers is the problem. Most people will attempt to solve it by pushing and pulling. Their notion is that by exerting force they can compel the body to yield the desired effect. It is a mindless approach that bespeaks a body divided against itself and a mind and body that function as antagonists rather than as an intelligent, integrated, and harmonious whole.

In the following exercise we will gently but persuasively address our bodies—our muscles, our nervous system, our brain—utilizing a nonverbal language which will produce the results we want. Instead of attempting to coerce the body, we will communicate by means of progressively increasing but nonaggressive demands what it is that we wish, and we will observe that the body will respond much more readily to such an approach than it ever would to the use of force.

First of all, seat yourself comfortably on the floor. Think back a moment to an earlier chapter where you recalled, or perhaps discovered, which of your two wrists was the more flexible, and try to remember how your hands felt then when you flexed and extended them. Flex and extend them now a few times, and see if the difference between the two wrists is about as you remembered it to be. With most people the right wrist is the more flexible, and the fingers of the right hand are also likely to move at least a little better. In this exercise we will work on the right hand and improve the mobility of the wrist and fingers and of the hand as a whole. However, the next time you do the exercise, reverse the instructions and work instead on the left hand. After that, alternate between the left hand and the right hand. Note that in the case of other exercises which work only with one side of the body, you should also alternate between working on the right side and the left.

Now rest your hands palms down on the floor. Think about how the fingers move individually and try to recall as vividly as you can those movements and, of course, the accompanying sensations. Then think about rapping first with the little finger of the right hand, then the next finger, and so on, until you are rapping with the thumb. One of your fingers is probably much less mobile than the others. Try by means of the imagined or recollected movements to determine which finger that is.

Now actually rap once, then twice, then three times, and then four times, with the thumb. Then do it with the index finger, then the middle finger, then the ring finger, and then the little finger, and see whether the least mobile finger is the one you thought it was. Have you learned something about your hand that you did not know before? It is your hand, and you use it countless times every day of your life. If you are unfamiliar with something so basic as the relative mobility of your own fingers, then what else might you not know about yourself? Remember that you have a greater awareness of your fingers than of almost any other parts of your body. What do you not know about those parts of your body of which you are least aware?

Now do that same rapping—one rap, then two, then three, then four—with the thumb, the middle finger, and the little finger; rap all three of them simultaneously. If it is difficult to do, then go slowly at first, then go more quickly as the movement becomes easier. Those fingers are very easy to move individually, so why should it be difficult to move the three of them at once? See if you can understand it.

Now let's make it a bit easier. Move just the ring finger and the little finger, rapping once, twice, three times, four times. See if you can do it without involving any of your other fingers (or your mouth, your breathing, etc.). When the fingers are differentiated as they should be, there is no movement except in the ones you want to move, and certainly there should be no movement in the other hand—although some people will find that the fingers of the other hand will also tend to move. This tendency is much more pronounced when one is working with movements of the toes. Then, when one or more toes of one foot are moved, you may find it very difficult to stop the same movement from occurring in the toes of the other foot and even in the fingers, although you will usually not be conscious of the superfluous movements unless they are brought to your attention.

Now go back to rapping with the thumb, the little finger, and the middle finger together, and do it a number of times. Then rap once, twice, three, and four times with the other two fingers and make certain that you are not holding your breath as you do so. Always try to breathe normally as you work and watch especially for the tendency to hold your breath when a little mental effort is being made. Now try rapping just the finger next to the little finger. That was the one that originally gave you the most trouble if you have a typical hand. It is probably now easier to move that finger than it was before.

Now try once more rapping the little finger, the middle finger, and the thumb, and see if that is getting any easier.

Now introduce the thumb of your left hand between the little finger and the next finger of your right hand. Let the thumb slide in a little ways, so that the fleshy part of the hand below the knuckle of the thumb is between the two fingers, and sense how it fits there. Now put that same fleshy part of your left hand between the ring finger and the middle finger of your right hand, and note how it fits. Then drop it into the space between the middle finger and the index finger. And then put it into the space between the index finger and the thumb of the right hand. Remember the sensations so that later you will be aware of how much more easily the hand fits between the various fingers, indicating that the space between them is wider—and the fingers more flexible.

Now take your left little finger and slide it between the right little finger and the ring finger. Slide it in and out at least twenty-five times. Then put the left little finger between the right ring and middle fingers and slide it in and out twenty-five times or more. Repeat the process with the right middle and index fingers and finally the right thumb and index finger.

Now do the same thing again, this time using the ring finger of your left hand. Slide it in and out twenty-five or thirty times between each finger of the right hand.

Repeat the entire procedure, using first the left middle finger, then the left thumb. Use the thumb just as you have used the fingers.

When you have finished doing that, introduce the fleshy part of the hand below the left thumb successively between the fingers of the right hand. Slide it in and out of each of the spaces between the fingers twenty-five or thirty times. It doesn't matter if the movement is in the right hand, the left hand, or both, so long as the hand keeps sliding in and out between the fingers—and so long as you know which hand, or hands, is moving.

Now introduce the side of your left wrist between the ring and little fingers of your right hand. Let the left wrist slide in and out successively between the fingers of the right hand, with the same number of repetitions as before. Then, when you have reached the space between the right thumb and index finger, slide your thumb and finger from the left wrist all the way up the forearm. Then repeat the movement, passing the forearm between all the fingers of the right hand. If a shirt or any garment you are wearing impedes the movement, try doing it with a bare arm.

Now try it with your lower leg—a bare leg is best. Insert the ankle between the ring and little finger of the right hand. Move the right hand up and down the shin bone, between the ankle and the knee, twenty-five or thirty times. Then do it with the next two fingers of the right hand, and so on.

When you have reached the space between the thumb and index finger and completed the series of movements, slide your hand up past your knee and see whether your thigh will now fit between the thumb and index finger. Make the movements up and down the length of your upper leg. Do the same with the next two fingers, and continue until you have completed the movements with the ring and little finger. Let your whole thigh pass between your fingers, or as much of it as you can manage without undue forcing.

Now just drop the fleshy part of the left hand beneath the thumb several times into each of the spaces between the fingers of the right hand. Also slide it in and out several times, and see if the spaces between the fingers have widened. Move the fingers of the right hand and notice whether they are now more flexible. Move the fingers of the right hand and flex the wrist.

Do the same with the left hand and compare the flexibility. You may feel a tingling in your right hand—a sensation you might describe as "energy."

Now rest a while on your back. Sense the difference between the two sides of your body and notice if the length feels different on the two sides. Whether you sense it or not, the length will be different. The repeated movement, with focused attention, of even one part of the body—the fingers, or an eye—will lengthen the muscles on that side. This is important, since it means that even a bedridden, nearly immobilized person can still do effective exercise, bringing about changes in some respects greater and possibly more important than the ones most people achieve by doing vigorous calisthenics.

Now sit up and take hold of the thumb of the right hand with the left hand and pull the thumb out so as to lengthen it while also rotating it gently. Do not, of course, "pop" the joint. Pull it away from its base and rotate it twenty-five times or so in a clockwise and then a counterclockwise direction. Do the same thing with the index finger, then the middle finger. Do the fingers move better when you rotate them clockwise or counterclockwise? See whether some fingers move better in one direction and some in the other direction. Move all your fingers successively in this way.

When you have finished with that, take hold of the thumb of the right hand near its base. Pull it a little and try to feel the articulation of the joint. See if you can feel the joint widening as you pull out. Then do the same thing with your other fingers.

Go back to the little finger and try to repeat the procedure with the joint nearest to the fingertip. Do the same thing with the other fingers.

Clench your left hand in a fist around your right thumb and then rotate the right wrist, keeping the left hand steady, so that the right hand rotates around its thumb. Do the movement many times, and then do it with all the fingers.

Let your hands rest palms downward on your thighs. Stroke the right thigh with the right hand, and then stroke the left thigh with the left hand. Sense whether one hand is lighter and at the same time touches more completely. Which hand would you rather be touched by?

Now you should know that the notion of a heavy-handed approach is more than a metaphor. It makes a difference in the sensing explorations of the hand when it touches something more completely. It can also make a great difference to whatever—and whoever—is being touched. Lie down and rest a minute. While you are lying there, scan your body for changes.

Sit up again in a comfortable position. Take hold of the small finger of your right hand and see now if you can make it ripple instead of just pulling it. Instead of an angular movement, it should be more of a serpentine movement, as if the finger is not impeded by the bones as it usually is. Try to make the finger ripple as if the bones are rubbery. Try it with each of your fingers.

Now, once again, compare your two hands and see whether the right hand and wrist are comparatively more flexible.

Altering One Side to Reeducate the Whole Body

ONE OF THE MORE INTERESTING and effective teaching techniques employed by Feldenkrais is that of improving the functioning of one side of the body while leaving the other side in its ordinary state. This allows for a striking comparison between what is and what could and should be—a demonstration the nervous system learns from and can act upon, in time making permanent the better, more pleasurable way of being, effecting the change in both sides of the body, not just one side. The comparison is also instructive to the conscious mind, enabling it to savor all the more appreciatively the knowledge that a greater realization of individual potential is possible. Mind and body are both educated and better enabled to pursue the common goals.

The following exercise applies that technique as well as other objectives of the Psychophysical Reeducation method. Body mechanics are taught in a practical way through immediate experience; mobility is increased, and the body image is brought closer in correspondence with the objective self.

To begin with, walk barefoot around the room for a while and observe your walking as closely as you can. In particular, compare the movement in the two legs, especially in the hip joints, the knees, the ankles, and the feet. Try to notice whether the movement is the same in the right and left legs, or whether one side moves better in some or all respects. Does one foot fall more lightly than the other, or does it seem to you that they are equal? As you walk, pay attention to the arm and shoulder movements. Note the sensations of movement in the shoulders and the elbows, and whether one arm swings in a larger arc or otherwise moves differently. When you turn, do you turn with equal ease to either side? If the arm and shoulder movements are better on one side, then again observe the leg movements. They are likely to be somewhat better on the side where the upper-body movements are better. In any case, be assured that you will be able to discriminate between the two sides as we continue.

Lie down on your back and scan your body, forming a clear picture of how it lies, and examine the clarity of the parts of the body image. Do the left and right sides lie equally, with equal pressure and contact with the floor? Note the backs of the legs, the buttocks, the sides of the back, and the shoulders. How far does each foot turn out to one side? Notice that if the feet are turning out to the sides, the legs must also be turning out, rotating from the hips.

Move the outside of the right foot toward the floor, then bring the foot back until it points straight up. Continue with that movement until you have done the usual twenty-five or so repetitions, or fewer if you find that difficult. The outside of the right foot should touch the floor on the right, or at least go in the direction of the floor. As you rotate the foot, be aware that the leg is rotating, and pay attention to the movement in the hip joint. Then stop and rest.

Bend the right leg so that it stands on the right foot, the knee pointing up to the ceiling. Let the right leg sink over to the right, so that if you were to touch the floor, the entire right side of the leg would make contact with the floor. Let the right leg lean over to the right toward the floor, as far as it will go easily, and then bring it back to the left, so that it stands on the foot and the top of the knee points up. (Figure 6.) Continue that movement with the right leg and notice that your right foot leans over on its side. As the leg goes over to the right, observe whether the left buttock rises a little, and part of the left upper leg. What is the lower left leg doing? Does the left foot go right when the right leg sinks right? Sense whether the left shoulder, the back on the left side, and the neck are moving. Is the movement greater on the right side or the left side of the neck, and how do they differ? What happens in the right shoulder, in the right arm and right side of the back? Sense simultaneously the right and

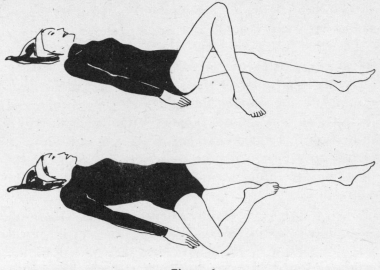

Figure 6

left sides, the whole back up to the shoulders, as you drop the leg over to the right and then bring it up again. Try to sense the back and the shoulders and the arms, the hands, the neck, the face and eyes. After that, rest a while.

Put the right leg down and extend it, like the left leg. Note how the body's right side lies, as you compare it to the left side. See whether the right side feels longer and try to determine if, in fact, it is longer. Pay attention to the sensations in the right side of the face, the right eye, the cheek, the right side of the mouth as compared to the left. Open your eyes a moment and see if you are looking somewhat to the right. Close your eyes and once again let your extended leg rotate over to the right, so that the outside of the foot approaches the floor. Keep bringing it back until the foot points up, then rotate it over to the right again.

Let the right foot rest with the toes pointing up. Then rotate it to the left as far as you can without straining, the inside of the foot approaching the floor on the left side. Rotate the leg as well. Then rotate the leg back, so that the foot points straight up again. Continue with that movement. See if now the right buttock comes up a little, with the right side of the back and the shoulder lifting to facilitate the movement. Then stop and rest.

Bend the right leg again so that it stands on the foot. This time let it drop over to the left, however far it will go. Then bring it back until the knee points to the ceiling. (Figure 7.) Pay attention to the movement and to the sensation in the hip joint. Feel what the whole pelvis does, and what happens in the left hip joint as you move. Now, if your leg is prevented from going

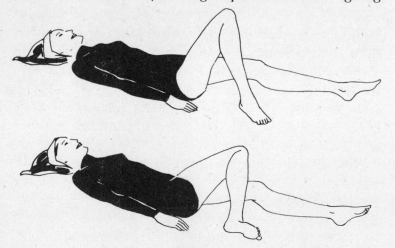

Figure 7

farther by the way the left leg is lying, try to figure out how the left one could lie to allow a larger movement of the right leg. Even if the right leg doesn't touch the left one, put the left leg someplace to increase the extent of the movement of the right leg. One thing you can do is move the left leg farther to the left. Try that, and then try bending it so that the left heel is resting near your bottom. Try both of those methods as you continue to move the right leg to the left and back. A third way would be to bend the left leg so that the left foot stands on the floor and then move it farther to the left. Just move it out of the way so that the right leg can tilt to the left more easily. As it does so, the left leg can tilt to the left, as it should be doing spontaneously, so that the whole pelvis rotates to the left and then back.

Now stop a moment. Put the left leg back down on the floor, extended, and continue dropping the right leg to the left. See if now the left leg is intelligent enough to get out of the way of the right leg spontaneously, and whether the whole pelvis rotates left more freely, with the upper body joining in the movement, the head turning to the left as the leg goes left and the right shoulder coming up. You can let the left knee bend a little, if it is not bent already, and see whether that allows you to move even more freely. Stop.

Now let the right leg drop over to the right side. Bend the left leg also, so that its foot stands on the floor, and let the right leg drop to the right again. Notice how that movement goes. Extend the left leg and let the right leg drop right. See if the movement keeps getting easier and easier. Then take a rest.

Note whether the right side of your body feels larger than the left—longer and fuller, more alive, more clearly in the body image. Say a few words to yourself. Ask: *Which side is more clearly in the body image?* Say it aloud several times: *Which side is more clearly in the body image?* As you ask that question, note whether you are tending to talk through the right side of your mouth. Observe, and try to talk directly through the middle. Then let your speech come out as it will, carefully observing what your mouth does.

Now bend both legs so that the feet stand on the floor. Draw your right leg up toward your chest a few times, the knee moving in toward the head, the top of the thigh approaching the rib cage. Then let the leg back down, so that the foot stands on the floor. Bring the leg up toward the chest again, then let it back down until the foot makes contact with the floor, and keep doing that movement. (Figure 8.) As you do it, sense

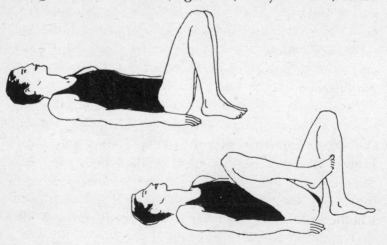

Figure 8

what happens to the hip joint, the shoulders, the head, and the neck. See whether, when the foot is going back toward the floor, your chin comes closer to your chest, and when the knee moves back toward the head, the chin moves away from the chest. Move the leg back and forth, allowing the movement of the head to be free. Do not voluntarily move the head; it will move by itself if you are not blocking the movement. Then stop and rest, leaving the legs standing.

Compare the right foot's contact with the floor with that of the left foot. Note which one senses the floor better. Is that because the contact with the floor is more complete on the right side, indicating that some of the tension has gone out of the foot?

Now make some circles with your right knee. To do it, lift the right foot off the floor just a little. Continue making circles with your right knee—small circles and then bigger and bigger circles, some circles made slowly and some quickly. Do some in one direction and then some in the opposite direction—big ones and small ones, slow ones and fast ones, slow big ones and fast small ones, slow small ones and fast big ones. And then rest.

Make circles again with your right knee and make them as big as you are able to. Gradually expand the size of the circles, so that they keep getting bigger and bigger. Are the circles larger, smaller, or is there any difference at all when you move clockwise? Does it make any difference what you do with your left leg—whether you bring it closer to the pelvis, move it farther away, or extend it? If you cannot do more than a few circles without causing pain in your hip, then do only what you can. Make very small circles, if that helps. Stop and imagine making circles, recalling the movement as vividly as possible.

Extend both legs and take a rest. Let the right foot rotate toward the floor on the right side, then bring it back so that the foot points straight up. Do the movement quickly while breathing normally, freeing the movement of any trace of compulsiveness. See how quick you can make it as you pay attention to the hip joint, letting the hip move as freely as possible.

Now rotate the leg to the left, so that the inside of the right foot approaches the floor. Bend your left leg and let it stand as you continue turning the right leg in. See if that facilitates the movement. Now let the right foot flop back and forth, as far to the right as it will go, and as far to the left. Let the left leg continue to stand, and allow the body to move as freely as it likes. The left leg may move freely, but the impetus should come from the movement of the right leg. Put the left leg down and extend it, continuing the movement with the right leg. See if you can now rotate the right leg and foot about as well as you could when the left leg was standing. Let the upper body participate as you move. Then stop and rest.

Now, one more time, bend both legs so that the feet are standing on the floor. Let the right leg drop to the right a few times. Then let the left leg down and extend it. Again, let the right leg drop to the right several times. Move the left leg out of the way and let the right leg drop to the left. Bend the left leg, the foot standing on the floor, and let the right leg keep dropping to the left. Extend the left leg and again let the right leg drop to the left. Bend the left leg, the foot flat on the floor, and bring the right leg back toward your chest a few times. Make a few circles with the right knee. Then put both legs down, extended.

Observe once more how you are lying and compare the two sides of your body. Especially note how the pelvis and legs are lying. Then slowly roll to one side and get up. Walk around the room for a while. Compare the two sides of your body as you walk. See whether the right side moves better and even tries to walk faster than the left side. The right leg may glide along, its momentum somewhat carrying the left leg. Note whether the right knee bends more, and also note the movements of the arms and shoulders as you walk. Observe your turning when you turn to the right and to the left.

Stand for a moment and, with feet in place, turn to the right and to the left. Note whether, when you turn to the right, the head, the neck, and even the eyes turn more freely and farther to the right. The work was done mainly on the hip joint, but probably the entire side has been affected. The muscles in the back on the right side are longer, so that the spine can twist better in that direction. The foot and the toes on the right side have improved, while those on the left side have stayed the same as before. Think about the interrelatedness of parts of the body—how a localized movement on one side can alter the entire side's functioning. The next time you do the exercise, work on the left side, substituting "right" for "left" and "left" for "right" in the instructions.

In your present state it would be an easy matter to

improve your body's left side. With a few actual or even imaginary movements it will quickly match the improvement in the right side. However, it better serves the purpose of reeducating the nervous system and the sensory mechanisms to let the differences remain so that they can be compared.

Releasing Tension in the Tongue

In the course of a complete reeducation program, one works with many parts of the body which are wholly ignored in conventional exercise programs. The following exercise illustrates how one such body part, the tongue, can be worked with. Eventually, you should be able to create exercises for yourself, applying the psychophysical method to parts of the body we cannot deal with here.

It is important for you to work with your body as completely as possible. It should be recognized that exercises such as this one—and most of the others, for that matter—can be especially important for rehabilitation and therapy. This exercise, in fact, was created to help relieve speech problems resulting from muscle spasms of the tongue. However, everyone can benefit from doing it.

The tongue is one of the most common sites of chronic unconscious muscular tension. Tensions in the tongue are likely to contribute to tensions in other parts of the face, including the muscles of the jaw. Among the detrimental effects can be a greater or lesser impairment of speech and interference with breathing. Only when the tongue is clearly in the body image will you be sufficiently aware of the excess tensions to be able to release them permanently.

Many people are conscious of tension in their jaws. This tension, if too severe, can eventually damage the jaw bones and do injury to the teeth. People who regularly gnash their teeth while awake or asleep have too much tension in the jaw, the tongue, the neck, and various muscles of the face. The release of the habitual tension in the tongue will begin to break up this entire tension pattern.

Some tension in the jaw and the muscles generally is, of course, desirable. If the jaw were completely relaxed, it would hang in the slack-jawed manner associated with idiots and victims of certain injuries. Ideally the jaw is sufficiently tensed for the upper teeth to almost make contact with the lower ones, just a little to the rear of the upper teeth. Even as you think about this you will become aware of the effort—which is usually unconscious—that you normally expend to keep the jaw from hanging too loosely. If the tongue is free of abnormal tension, it will lie relaxed on the floor of the mouth, its tip making very slight contact with the backs of the teeth. Now we will try to release any tensions in the tongue that prevent it from lying in the mouth as it should and by this means also try to effect some relaxation of the musculature of the jaw, lower face, and neck.

To begin, sit in a comfortable position, holding the head reasonably erect. Scan your tongue, the whole surface of it insofar as you can. Sense its position in relation to the roof and to the floor of your mouth. See whether it touches your teeth in the front. Is it in the middle or is it closer to the left cheek or to the right cheek?

Sense the bottom of it, the top of it, how wide it is, how long it is, how thick it is. See whether you notice any tension in it and whether it seems to change as you examine it. Does it get any wider or bigger? Are you more aware of the inside of your mouth as you bring the tongue more fully into your awareness?

Now, run the tip of your tongue over the inside of your lower teeth a few times. Go as far from left to right and right to left as you can. And then, just for a moment, run your tongue over the tops of the lower teeth. Then over the cutting edges of the upper teeth and the insides of the upper teeth, as far to the left and as far to the right as you can.

Next run your tongue over the outside of the upper teeth, between the teeth and the upper lip, going from left to right as far as you can. Do the same with the lower teeth, running your tongue between the teeth and the lower lip. Do each of the movements at least ten or fifteen times.

Stop. Now press your tongue against the roof of

your mouth. Press hard and hold it there for a while. Breathe normally as you do it. Relax, let go, and then press again. Relax, and then press your tongue against the floor of your mouth. Do it in such a way that as your tongue presses, your mouth opens. You should be pushing your lower jaw down with your tongue. Push it down as far as it will go. Do this several times.

Now press your tongue against the roof of the mouth so that you have the feeling that you are pushing the mouth open. Do it several times.

Now close your mouth and see whether you feel any tension in the jaw or the facial muscles. Then yawn deeply several times. Try to be aware of your tongue as you yawn. Is it difficult to keep track of the position of your tongue when you are yawning? Now just open your mouth several times to see how wide you can open it without any strain. Stop and thrust your lower jaw forward so that your lower teeth come out in front of your upper teeth and lip. Do it several times.

Try opening your mouth again to see if it opens wider now and then flick your tongue from left to right a few times. Flick it in and out between your lips, like a snake, several times. Then lie down on your back and rest.

As you rest, try to become aware of the tongue again, whether it is positioned in the mouth differently than it was when you were sitting. Is it farther back in the mouth now and farther away from your teeth? How about the distances between the tongue and the roof of the mouth and the tongue and the floor of the mouth? Are they the same as before or different? Is the tongue generally in the middle of the mouth? Try to remember how it was when you were sitting up and compare that with how it is now.

If you can't remember, sit up for just a moment and see how the tongue lies. See whether it is closer to the floor of the mouth and to the teeth and notice any other differences. Then lie down again and examine it. Are you becoming more clearly aware of the tongue than you were before?

Now roll your head from side to side several times and see what happens to the tongue. See whether when you roll the head to the right the tongue goes to the right side, and when you roll the head to the left the tongue goes to the left without any effort on your part. Roll your head way over to the left and observe where the tongue goes. Then way over to the right, again observing where the tongue goes.

Do it with your eyes open and with your eyes closed. See whether that makes any difference. Do it with the eyes open and look as far to the side as you can. When you look to the front, focus as far away as possible. When you look to the right side again look as far as you can. Does that make any difference in the movement of the tongue as compared to what it was when you did it with your eyes closed?

Pull your chin down toward your chest as far as it will go easily. Close your mouth and rest a moment. Then just move the tongue from left to right. Move it toward the left cheek, then toward the right cheek, back and forth like a pendulum, breathing freely as you do it. Now run your tongue, from right to left, over the outside of your upper teeth, between the teeth and the lip, then over the outside of the lower teeth, between the teeth and the lip.

Next, use your tongue to explore the inside of your mouth for a time. Go everywhere you can with it. Sense the difference between the way the front of the teeth feels to you and the way the back of the teeth feels, the difference between the roof and the floor of the mouth, and how the insides of the cheeks feel.

Try it first with the jaw closed tight, then with the mouth open a little. Still exploring with the tongue, open the mouth wide. Then close it tightly once again, continuing to move the tongue around. Does the tongue feel a little cramped now, maybe even a bit claustrophobic in such a narrow space?

Now yawn deeply several times, observing the tongue as you do it. Take a little rest. Observe how the tongue lies. Do you notice any difference in its width? in its length? If your tongue was far back behind the teeth when you began, it should be considerably longer and wider now that the tension has gone out of it. If your tongue was just a bit back from the teeth when you first lay down, it may now want to poke out between the teeth somewhat.

Now, sit up again. Stick your tongue out a little and hold it there with your teeth to mark how far out it extends. Then stick it out just a little more, again biting down gently with the teeth to measure your progress. Keep doing this, sticking your tongue out a little farther each time. Extend it, hold it, then extend it a little more.

When you've gone as far as you can, retract your tongue and repeat the process, breathing normally as you do it. See how many little extensions you can make, whether you can extend it ten times, fifteen times, or twenty times, putting it out just a little farther each time. All your movements should be light and gentle.

Now stop and retract your tongue. Then stick it out as far as is comfortable. Keeping your tongue rigid, move it in circles. You should be circling with your whole head. You can imagine that you're using your tongue to push the hand of a clock around the dial. First turn the hand clockwise around the dial, then turn it counterclockwise.

Stop and move your tongue in and out of your mouth, using your lips to sense what the tongue feels like. Try to do it so that the tongue doesn't scrape over your teeth. First sense primarily the top side of the tongue and the upper lip as you move it in and out. Then sense the lower side of the tongue and the lower lip. Compare the great difference between the top of the tongue and the bottom of the tongue. Then sense both the top and the bottom simultaneously as the tongue goes in and out.

With the tongue still protruding, move it from side to side, from one corner of the mouth to the other. See whether you can sense the difference between the top and the bottom of the tongue as clearly when it goes from side to side.

Dart the tongue in and out between the lips several times, scraping the teeth very gently as you do it.

Now move the tongue in an oval over the gums, between the teeth and lips. Circle round and round in one direction, in the other direction, and then stop.

Now, get down on your hands and your knees for a moment. Look at the floor and sense how the tongue hangs. Open your mouth and let the tongue dangle. Raise your head up and down a few times with the tongue hanging out. See whether it touches the lower lip when the head comes up and the upper lip when the head goes down.

Shake your head from side to side a few times and see if you can let the tongue swing freely as your head moves. Then stick it out and pull it in a few times while looking at the floor. Can you see your tongue as it comes out of your mouth? Watch it as it appears and as it retracts.

Move your tongue from side to side and note whether you can continue to see it. Make clockwise and counterclockwise circles with your tongue, still looking at it if you can. Then just move the tongue in and out again.

Sit back down and observe once more how your tongue lies in your mouth. Does it seem wider, flatter, and longer? Are you more clearly aware of the inside of your mouth and your lips now? See if you can sense clearly where your lips touch each other. Open and close your mouth several times. Your mouth should open very easily now.

Lie down on your back and roll your head from side to side several times. Do it a number of times with your eyes closed and a number of times with your eyes open, going way over to one side and then the other. Try it with your arms folded on your chest and see whether the tongue goes easily and naturally from one side to the other. As you move your head from side to side consciously increase the speed and movement of the tongue inside the mouth. The tongue should move easily and without compulsion, like a very fast pendulum.

Stop. Dart your tongue in and out of your mouth and see whether it moves very quickly now. Move it back and forth between the corners of your mouth and see how quickly that goes.

Sit up and stick your tongue out several times, noticing the difference in your sensing of the top and the bottom of the tongue. Does the tongue go out more easily and farther now? Is it more relaxed? Retract your tongue and note now how it lies on the floor of the mouth. Is its tip just behind the teeth now? Does the tongue seem wider than before? Get up and walk around a little and continue to make your observations. Keep the tongue clearly in your awareness and resolve to remember what you are now sensing.

Objective Movements in Subjective Realities

THE FOLLOWING EXERCISE will increase the ease and range of the movement in the elbows while demonstrating some of the techniques of Psychophysical Reeducation. For instance, the results obtained will be enhanced by blending actual movements with subjective realities: environments of the mind. The body will play in imagination's playground—the gymnasium which best serves the body's needs because it can be exactly what you want it to be, offering any equipment you like, any amount of space.

Simple movement does not at all guarantee greater flexibility of the elbows. A person can hammer, or beat a drum, or row, or unreel a rope without any noticeable effect on the elbows (except, possibly, stiffness due to strain or fatigue). Any of those activities *could,* however, enhance elbow flexibility, but only if done with the proper attitude, intention, and focused attention, leading to increasing awareness.

Sit down on the floor with your legs in front of you, preferably in some Oriental-type position which you can sustain without shifting too often for the next half hour or so. The soles of the feet might be brought together in Japanese fashion, or the legs might be brought closer to the body in an approximation of one of the yoga positions. Once you have become familiar with one of these ways of sitting, you will find that it can be maintained for far longer periods of time with greater comfort and less movement than any sitting position commonly used in Western countries.

Each of the movements we will describe should be performed fifteen to thirty times, depending upon what is comfortable for you, and each sequence of movements should be completed in about thirty seconds. Avoid any undue strain or discomfort and if you need to stop and rest a bit, do so, but during your pause, continue to imagine performing the movement. This imagining should be kinesthetic as well as visual, including all the sensations involved.

First extend your arms out to the sides at shoulder height and bend the elbows so that the lower arms and the hands are dangling. Then let the hands and the lower arms swing freely from the elbows, the hands first approaching each other, then moving away from each other. Breathe freely as they swing and observe the sensations in your body. (Figure 9.)

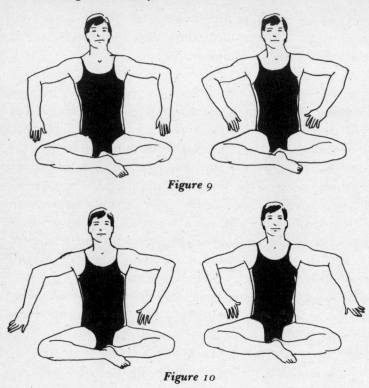

Figure 9

Figure 10

Now let the hands and arms swing so that both of them move simultaneously to the left and then back to the right, the distance between them remaining approximately the same. (Figure 10.)

Put your arms down and rest a bit.

Now just bend your right arm a few times. Flex and extend it, and try to sense what it is that happens in the elbow. Do the same thing for a while with the left arm. Take hold of your left elbow with your right hand and try to sense with the hand what is happening while you bend your elbow.

Stop and once again flex and extend your right arm, feeling the movements in the right elbow with the left hand. Holding the elbow, rotate your arm from left to right, so that first the back of the hand is up and then the palm. If you could observe your skeleton, you would see that one of the long bones in the forearm is now moving around the other, larger bone. If you have a chance to observe this movement later in a skeleton, do so; a great deal about the body's movement potential can be learned from studying skeletal movements unimpeded by muscles and other body tissues.

Still holding your right elbow with your left hand, make some circles with the right hand and forearm. Circle in one direction and then in the other, sensing with your hand any movement in the elbow.

Take hold of the left elbow with your right hand and use that hand to flex and extend the left arm. Move the left arm in all directions, exploring the elbow further with your hand.

Now lie down on your back and rest.

Sense your body as it lies there on the floor. For at least a minute scan its surface, noting especially the contact of the body with the floor and whether the two sides of the body lie evenly.

Sense the contact the elbows make with the floor. Then extend your arms out to the sides at shoulder height. Bend both of your arms at the elbows so that the palms of the hands lie on your chest. Raise your forearms so that they extend toward the ceiling and then bring them down again so that the palms make contact with the chest. When you have done this fifteen to thirty times (more if you can do so easily), repeat the movement, this time touching the chest with the thumb side of the hand instead of the palms.

Continue the movement, first bending the elbows so that the sides of the hand with the little finger touch the chest, then bending them so that the backs of the hands touch the chest, or come as close to it as possible. Remember, each of these sequences should last for about thirty seconds. (Figure 11.)

Figure 11

Lie with your arms extended at shoulder height. Now bend the arms at the elbows and lower them so that the backs of the hands touch the floor. When you have done this a number of times, repeat the sequence, first with the palms touching the floor, then with the

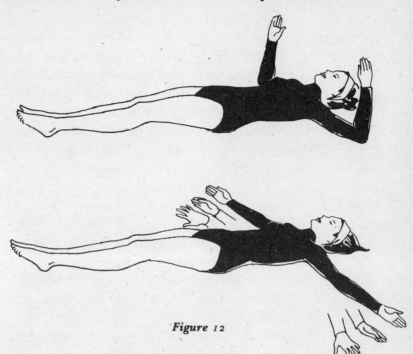

Figure 12

little-finger sides of the hands touching the floor, and finally with the thumb sides of the hands touching the floor. Stop and rest a minute. (Figure 12.)

Now reach over your chest and take hold of your elbows with your hands. Holding the elbows, move the arms from side to side so that they approach the ground first on the left side and then on the right.

Let your head go with the movement for a while, your head and eyes following your elbows to the left, then back over to the right. Next fix your glance on some point on the ceiling, so that the head no longer moves, and continue the movement of the arms from side to side.

Now keeping the head fixed, let your eyes follow the movement of your elbows. Try to follow your elbows visually as far as you can. Then let the head and eyes go together with the arms. Do the movement for a while holding your forearms instead of your elbows. Then hold the wrists. And take a little rest.

Now put both your hands a little below your chest on your rib cage and flap the elbows like wings, lifting them toward the ceiling, then lowering them to the floor.

Move your hands up a little so they lie on your chest. Now flap the arms in a different direction, so they come down against your body with the inside of your elbows lightly striking your rib cage. Make the range of that flapping as extensive as you can without straining.

Leaving the hands on the chest, bring the elbows out to the sides and make circles with them. Make a number of circles forward and then a number backward. Pretend that you are drawing circles on something with your elbows and imagine what those circles look like. Stop and rest a minute.

Now extend your arms out to your sides at shoulder height and bend your arms at your elbows so both hands point to the ceiling. Make circles with your hands, in one direction for a while, and then in the other direction. Make small circles, and then, gradually, bigger ones.

Make more small circles with quick agile movements. Then make bigger ones with the same fast movement. Make small slow circles and then large slow ones. From time to time reverse the direction of the circles while moving at different speeds.

Stop, but leave the arms bent and the hands pointed upward. Move your hands as if you were stirring something. For a while imagine stirring something that is thick and heavy. Then imagine stirring something very thin that offers no resistance and see if your arms move differently. Now stop and rest.

With the arms still bent, rap with your elbows on the floor. See how you have to arrange your arms in order to rap touching just the tips of your elbows to the floor. When you have done that for a while, alternate the rapping between the left and the right elbows. (Figure 13.)

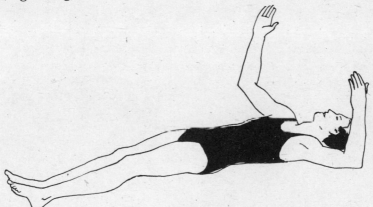

Figure 13

Now imagine that you are holding a broom handle or a long stick with both hands. Push it up with your arms extending and then bring it down, so that the elbows touch the floor. Now imagine you are lifting something quite heavy, something that would offer considerable resistance, like the barbell a weightlifter uses. Imagine the barbell at different weights and see what it feels like. Then lift a light broom handle or a long stick again. Now put your arms down and rest. (Figure 14.)

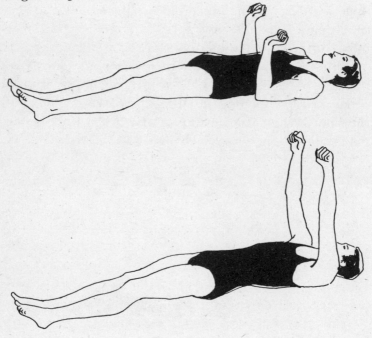

Figure 14

Imagine that suspended over the middle of your body somewhere is a door that you are to knock on with your fists. Pound on the door with your fists—first one fist, then the other one. Do that for a while, then rap on the door simultaneously with both fists. Then alternate fists again. Bring the door closer to you and rap. Now move it farther away than it was at the start and once again rap on the door. Stop.

Now imagine that there is a big spool of rope attached to the ceiling someplace beyond the bottom of your feet and that you can take hold of the end of the rope with your two hands. Reach up with one hand, then the other, unreeling the rope as you pull it toward you. At first the rope offers some resistance and you have to pull fairly hard to unreel it. As you continue, the resistance diminishes so that the rope becomes much easier to unreel. Keep pulling until the rope ceases to offer any resistance at all. Notice how quickly and easily your arms are moving.

Imagine now that the rope is somewhere on the ceiling to the rear of you, so that you have to reach back over your head to pull it. Then imagine that the rope is once again beyond your feet and that as you unreel it, it offers no resistance whatever. Stop and rest.

Now imagine that on either side of you there is a little wall and that when you reach out you can touch the walls. Reach out and rap on both of the walls with your fists. Rap as lightly or as vigorously as you like. Rap simultaneously with both fists, then alternately with one fist after the other. You can rap slowly or quickly, and you can vary the speed from one fist to the other. Experiment with different combinations.

Try rapping with the backs of your hands for a while, then with the sides of your hands where the small finger is. Rap many times with the tips of your fingers. Make circles with the tips of your fingers on the surface of the wall, then with the tip of just the little finger. Poke the wall gently with your middle finger only.

Now imagine that you are lying under a table with the surface just above you and knock gently on that with your fists. Knock simultaneously with both fists and alternately with one fist, then the other. Stop and take a short rest.

Now imagine that there is a little table just a few inches above your chest and that you want to rap on the top of it with the palm of your hand. Rap on the table top slowly for a while and then see how quickly you can rap. Note whether you are breathing normally as you do the movements.

Extend your arms out to your sides at shoulder height. Bend the elbows so that the forearms point to the ceiling and let the hands dangle from the wrists. Make many small circles with the hands, making sure that the wrists, hands, and elbows are very loose and free. Circle in one direction for a while and then in the other direction.

Make circles of many different sizes and vary the speed at which you make them. Make big circles with one hand while you make small circles with the other. Circle in one direction with one hand while you circle in the opposite direction with the other. Try making fast circles with one hand while you make slow ones with the other, alternating the fast and slow circles from one side of the body to the other. Try to vary simultaneously the size, the speed, and the direction of the circles in many different combinations. Experiment with that for a while. Then just do whatever you feel like doing, but sense the elbows very clearly as you continue to make various movements. Put your arms down and have a rest.

Now, a few more times, reel in the rope. Do this quickly and sense whether the movement is different now from the first time you did it. Is it different in the elbows? in the shoulders? Sense the two shoulder blades, how one comes down and the other goes up as you reel in the rope. Reel it in very quickly now, *as though it offered no resistance,* and with the elbows *very free.* Stop.

Now once again take hold of your elbows with your hands and move your arms from side to side, sensing how the elbows bend now. Then rest.

As you rest, just bend the arms wherever they are lying and make a few circles with the forearms and hands. Keep the wrists limp and let the hands wave loosely in the air. Stop again.

Now slowly sit up with your legs in front of you in an Oriental-type position. Extend your arms to the sides at shoulder height and bend them, letting the forearms swing freely. Then put your hands in your lap. Alternately flex and extend your arms, sensing your elbows as you do that.

Lie back down and take your left elbow in your right hand. Move your left arm a little and sense what the elbow feels like with your hand. Rotate your arm. Bend it. See what you feel.

Change over, holding the right elbow with the left hand, sensing the movement in the elbow as you make different movements with your arm. See if the elbow is clear now to your touch, clearer than it was at the beginning.

Put your hands on your chest and your arms on the floor and try to sense both elbows clearly at the same time.

Get up and walk around, letting your arms swing free, and see what that feels like. See whether your elbows and shoulders now naturally swing more freely and with more movement. Stand in place and see how fast you can bend and extend your arms. Are they freer now than they were at the beginning?

On many occasions in the past you have doubtless engaged in activities that involved bending the elbows many times. But the movement of the elbows did not become any freer or quicker as a result. Try to understand why this time such changes occurred when they did not occur in the past.

Geriatric Applications

PSYCHOPHYSICAL REEDUCATION EXERCISES can be simple or complex, brief or extended, composed of very few movements or many. Examples of simple, brief exercises are those at the end of the chapter titled "An Introduction to Yourself." In general, the longer, more complicated exercises involving more movements will yield greater results. However, much can be accomplished with exercises which are relatively brief and simple and which require very little effort. They are excellent rehabilitation exercises and can be done with very striking results even by infirm elderly people. With the very elderly, motivation and concentration may be the stumbling blocks; the movements need not be a deterrent, especially if people follow the repeated instruction to do only what is well within one's present means.

The following exercise was created for Kay Masters, seventy-five-year-old mother of one of the authors. She did it easily and with benefit, even though she was then confined to a wheelchair with a minor fracture of her foot. She also did many other exercises, which were modified slightly to allow for her condition. Psycho-physical exercises are gradually finding their way into programs to improve the capacities and the lives of older people. They should be a revolutionary force.

To do this exercise, sit in a chair that is comfortable, but which has a firm back and bottom. Do not use a chair into which your body sinks. If the chair has arms, you will have to seat yourself far enough forward so that your legs and hips can move unimpeded according to the instructions given. Remember to do as many repetitions as you can do easily, up to twenty-five.

Figure 15

Move so that you are sitting at least halfway forward in (toward the front of) your chair. Spread your feet and legs a little wider than usual, the knees bent and the feet about parallel. Rest your hands where they will not obstruct your movements—they should not be resting on your legs. (Figure 15.)

Let your right leg drop over to the right, allowing the foot to tilt onto its right side, then bring it back until the bottom of the foot is once more flat on the floor. Continue to do this, finding a position in the chair that will let your leg move freely. Let the right leg drop right, then bring it back to the middle, paying attention to the movement in your hip joint. It should be an effortless movement. Note the sensations and breathe easily. (Figure 16.)

Figure 16

Stop for a moment. Then extend your right leg straight out in front of you. Rotate it so that the right foot tilts to the right, then bring it back. The foot

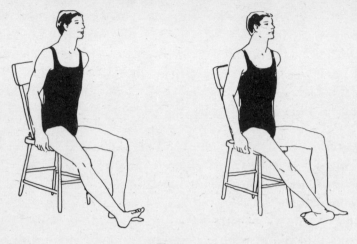

Figure 17

should turn on its heel with the rest of the foot off the floor. As you continue that movement, try to make it smoother, easier, more extensive. Just let the foot fall to the right, keeping the leg straight. (Figure 17.) Then bend your knee a little and try it. When you bend your knee, your foot must come closer to the chair. When the sequence is completed, take a rest.

Extend your right leg and try letting the foot fall to the left, so that the inside of the foot approaches the floor. (Figure 18.) Do that movement for a while. Bring the foot a little closer to the chair, so that the knee bends a little, and do it. Then stop and rest.

Extend the right leg straight out in front of you again and see if you can push the foot forward along the floor, and then draw it back toward you. The foot must be standing on its heel, and you should be sitting far enough forward in your chair for the leg to be

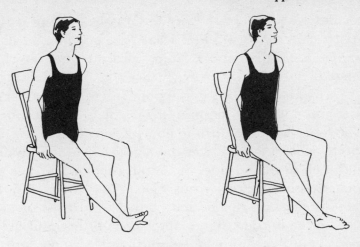

Figure 18

quite straight, with no bending at the knee. Keeping the leg straight, push the right heel forward, then bring it back, along the floor. Be careful not to fall off your chair—hold the arms or seat lightly with your hands. Let the right side of your body go with the movement. The right shoulder should move forward when the right leg goes forward, so that your body twists a little to the left. At the same time, the left shoulder will go back. This movement will become clearer to you as we continue.

Now spread your feet and legs a little and let your right leg fall to the left, to the inside. The leg will fall more easily if the foot is standing on its heel. Pay attention to what happens in the hip joint as the leg falls. Observe that the right buttock moves a little on the chair. Put your foot out a bit farther and continue with the movement. Then extend the leg out as far as it will go and let it fall to the inside. Watch the foot as it approaches the floor. Feel what happens now in the hip joint and the buttock. Stop, but leave your leg extended.

Turn the foot to the inside and then bring it back past the upright position and turn it to the outside. The foot should be turning on its heel with the rest of the foot off the floor. Let the leg rotate to the inside and then to the outside. Sense the rotation in the hip joint. Sense that when your foot rotates to the inside there is pressure on the left buttock, and when it rotates to the outside there is pressure on the right buttock. Your body should be shifting back and forth, from one side to the other, as you turn your foot. Be aware of the movement in your hip. Then, for just a second, pay attention to what is going on in the left hip joint. Quite a bit should be happening there, too. Now concentrate again on the right hip. With your heel only touching the floor, keep flopping your foot back and forth.

Stop and bring the right foot back until it stands about parallel with the left foot. Place it so that it won't bump the left leg, then let the whole leg flop from left to right. As the knee moves to the left, the foot will tilt onto its left side. As the knee moves to the right, the foot will tilt onto its right side. Try to make the movement smooth and easy. Bring your foot a bit closer to the chair. See how far you should place your foot from the chair in order to let the leg move most freely and most extensively. Is it at the point when the foot is almost at the chair, when the two feet are parallel, when the foot is a little farther out, or when the leg is extended? Experiment with different positions until you discover which one is best for this particular movement. When you have solved the problem, take a rest.

Shift your weight onto your left buttock so that the right one rises slightly off the chair. Then sink onto the right buttock and let the left buttock come up. Sense what happens in the hip joints as you do that. Can you sense more clearly what is happening in the right hip? See whether you move more easily to the right than to the left. Rest.

Extend your right leg out and raise your foot off the floor a little. If you sit all the way back in your chair, you will find that you can lift the leg higher and with greater ease. Then make some circles with your foot, keeping your leg stiff. Make some in one direction. Then make some in the other direction. You can stop and rest any time you get tired. Make little circles and then bigger circles. Make slow circles and then faster circles. See that you don't hold your breath. Put the leg down and rest.

Sitting far back in your chair, extend your right leg again and raise your foot off the floor. Just move the foot and leg from left to right, without rotating the hip or flopping the foot. Let the upper leg slide from side to side across the chair as the leg goes from left to right. Then, still holding the leg off the floor, do flop the foot left and right, turning it to the inside, then to the outside. Don't think about moving the whole leg now, just the foot. Then put your leg down and rest.

Lean forward, toward the edge of your chair. Extend the right leg, the foot standing on its heel. Slide the foot forward and back along the floor without bending the knee. Observe the difference in the way you are using your hip joint. Let your upper body, including your shoulders, move freely, the body twisting as the foot slides forward and back. Then rest a minute with both knees bent and both feet flat on the floor. Lift the right foot off the floor and put it down again, very lightly and easily. Do this many times. Extend the right leg and flop the foot from left to right without bending your knee. Make the lightest, easiest movement you can. Put your hand on your right hip and feel the movement there as the foot and leg go from left to right. Try to feel it clearly. The upper leg has one big bone and at the end is a knob which turns in the socket of your hip as your leg goes from left to right. Try to sense where the socket is. Feel the shifting of the weight of the body from side to side. What is happening to the left side of your rib cage?

Now just bend the leg normally so that the two feet stand side by side. Let the right knee go from left to right. See how it moves now. You should feel considerably greater freedom. Breathe in as you move the leg. Then try moving the leg as you breathe out. Put the foot a little farther out and move the leg from left to right. Then extend the leg completely and flop it from left to right. Note how your hip joint is turning now. A couple of times just slide the foot forward and backward, away from your pelvis, then back toward it. Keep your leg stiff, letting the movement come from the hip. Then stop and take a rest.

Now extend both of your legs. Lift the right leg several times. Then lift the left one. See whether the right leg is easier to lift, and whether it also lifts higher. Which leg feels heavier? After all of that work, you would think that the right leg would be tired, would feel heavier. Instead, it feels lighter and moves more easily than the left leg.

Get up and walk around a bit. Turn to the right and then to the left. In which direction do you turn better? Stand still and lift the right leg out to the front, keeping it straight. Then do the same thing with the left leg. Lift each leg out to the side. Notice that, without thinking about it, you make a larger movement with the right leg.

Next time you do this exercise, reverse the instructions and work with the left leg. After that, alternate working with the right and left sides.

A NOTE ON
THE FOLLOWING EXERCISES

In the following exercises the subjective component becomes more important and there is much less movement of the body in space. However, there will still occur pronounced changes in the body, as well as changes which are not so demonstrable. With some of these exercises we hope to extend psychophysical methods into areas that have not yet been thoroughly explored.

Previous remarks about the number of repetitions to be performed should now be ignored. Also, the following exercises do not need to be done with the same regularity as those which you have just completed. The preceding exercises should be done again and again if they are to bring about far-reaching changes in your body, your mind, and your functioning. What you do in the future with the following exercises, you yourself can best decide. Here, intuition and feeling may be the best guides when you are working on your own.

The following exercises also open up new avenues of research which are very little traveled. We will welcome hearing from readers who pursue these pathways. Those who push ahead far enough and for long enough should reach regions as yet uncharted.

Left Brain, Right Brain

IN THE PRECEDING EXERCISES we have seen that when some part of the body is worked with over a period of time and consciousness remains focused on that part, a definite improvement in the functioning of the part results. Moreover, with repeated exercise, the functioning is permanently improved and the part or parts of the body involved become healthier, stronger, more agile, better in almost every way. Anyone who continues to work with the exercises already provided in this book will realize such benefits insofar as the musculoskeletal systems of the body are concerned. We also have evidence from experience with the exercises that glandular functioning improves and that the nervous system benefits as well. Taking note of these facts, one then wonders whether it is not possible to use the method of the psychophysical exercises to work directly on the human brain to improve its health and functioning.

Just as certain joints or muscles have been the focus of attention in the earlier work, here attention is focused on the parts of the brain which are "exercised" in a variety of ways, and the brain remains the focal point of intention. As an effect of this focusing, most people will sense the interior of their skull and the surface of the brain probably for the first time in their lives. Some will feel that they can sense movement in the brain and even sense the brain transmitting and receiving signals to and from other parts of the body.

What are we to make of this experience of "sensing" the brain? It is the prevailing and rarely questioned belief that the brain cannot be sensed and that there is no means by which the brain and its physical processes could be brought into our awareness. If that belief is correct, then what is it that we are sensing in this exercise? One can only suppose that we are sensing changes in the flow of blood and in the condition of the muscles of the scalp and the neighboring regions. If that is so then this still might indicate some unusual stimulus in the brain, which then triggers those responses and accompanying sensations.

We may not wish to exclude completely the possibility that we do sense the brain and that those who maintain that such sensing is impossible are in error. However, there are also elements intentionally introduced into this exercise which seem to suggest that, at least a part of the time, what is being sensed is a kind of image of the brain, rather than the brain itself.

What matters most is not what we are sensing but whether the exercise is of value. If in fact we can exercise the brain directly, and so improve its health and its functioning, then this kind of exercise will constitute a discovery and a breakthrough.

Unfortunately, it is not as easy to determine the effects of these exercises on the brain as it is to determine the effects of exercises which work with the joints and the muscles of the body. Evidently as with, say, eye exercises, any changes are of a lesser magnitude, there are subtler but still noticeable changes in health and functioning, which may occur much more slowly so that improvement is more difficult to detect or measure objectively. The brain exercises should be experimentally tested on a large number of research subjects over a considerable period of time and with frequent and numerous experiences of the exercises. Only by such classical means will we arrive at conclusions acceptable to scientists, educators, and others whom we would wish to persuade in this case.

Such long-range and massive experimentation has not been carried out by us and so we can only speak of certain indications that repeated practice of the brain exercises may improve mental functioning.[1] We cannot speak of any possible improvement in the health of the brain, since we have had no way to obtain such evi-

[1] The authors and the Foundation for Mind Research will make more "brain exercises" available to those who seem to us to be serious and qualified researchers who will share their findings with us.

dence. Quite apart from these matters we have been discussing, the exercise has other objectives and gives other advantages. Most people afterward experience a rather deep state of relaxation and the exercise could be used for that purpose alone. The exercise has the additional purpose of bringing some parts of the head, especially the back of the head, more completely into the body image. This is important and well worth doing and we know only a few other means, if any, by which it can be so efficiently achieved. We have seen no hint that the exercises could be harmful, but we do not recommend them for psychotic individuals who might build fantasies around them.

We will now proceed to the exercise itself. Because it must be done with the eyes closed, it is difficult, although not impossible, to do it unassisted, working from the book. It is usually better to have someone read the instructions to you, being sure that he or she allows you sufficient time to carry out each segment of the exercise. It might be best if you yourself take charge of the timing and indicate, by moving a finger or by some other such signal, when you would like the next instruction read. As with the other exercises, you may also find that it works best for you to make your own tape recording and then play it back. You may wish to obtain the tape-recorded exercises mentioned at the end of the book.

Now seat yourself in some comfortable position which you will be able to maintain with minimal discomfort and without shifting for the next forty minutes or so. It is best if you can sit on the floor in some Oriental-type position. If that is not comfortable for you, then seat yourself as you prefer.

Now close your eyes and try to become as aware as possible of your left eye. Keeping your eyes closed, look down at the floor with your left eye. Look up toward the ceiling with it. Now look to the right with it, then look to the left. Try to be aware of the shape and the weight of your left eyeball.

Now do the same thing with the right eye. Keeping your eyes closed, look up and then down several times with your right eye, then to the right and to the left a few times.

Now shift your attention to the left side of your brain, above your left eye. You should be focusing on the space inside of the skull where the brain is. Do that for a few seconds.

Now shift your attention to the right side of your brain and keep it there a little while. Shift now to the left side, then bring it back to the right side again. Keep shifting your attention back and forth between the two sides of your brain.

A number of images will now be suggested to you, and you will either see them or you will just imagine as vividly as possible what they look like. Remember to keep your eyes closed while doing the exercises.

To begin with, look up at the left side of your brain and see or imagine there the number 1. Look over to the right side and see the letter A. Look left at the number 2 and then look right at the letter B. Next on the left is 3 and then on the right is C. On the left is 4

and on the right is D. On the left, 5, and on the right,
E. Continue on through the alphabet to Z and the
number 26 if you can, seeing the number on the left
and the letter on the right.

Now do it the opposite way. Look first to the right at
the number 1 and then to the left at the letter A. Now
2 is on the right and B is on the left. Continue on
through 26 and Z.

Think for a moment about what you just did and
whether you did it any better on one side than on the
other. If there was any significant difference, you
might want to work with the numbers and letters
frequently until you have equalized your performance
on the left and right sides.

Now, always with the eyes closed, look up toward the
left side of your brain and observe there, or imagine, a
joyous scene of a baby being born. On the right, picture an old person dying.

Let that image go and look left, at a group of Asian
monks in robes who are chanting and praying. On the
right there is a battlefield.

On the left is the sun; on the right is the moon.

On the left is a day in springtime; on the right is a
day in winter.

On the left is a hot summer day; on the right is a day
in autumn.

On the left is the color red; and on the right, the
color blue.

On the left it is green; and on the right it is yellow.

Now on the left, orange; and on the right, purple.

In addition to seeing or imagining what something

looks like, you can also imagine how it sounds or tastes or smells, or what it would be like to touch. Now, on the left side of your brain, imagine the sensation of touching velvet. Try to capture the feeling and breathe easily as you experience it. On the right, touch a piece of tree bark.

On the left, imagine the sensation of caressing silk. On the right, the feel of corrugated metal.

On the left, the feeling of sandpaper; on the right, that of slippery glass.

On the left, run your hands and fingers up and down the length of an icicle. On the right, put your hand into warm water.

Now, on the left, imagine the sound of someone bouncing a large ball. On the right, the sound of an airplane motor. On the left, the honking of a horn; on the right, bells tolling. On the left, machine-gun fire; on the right, the barking of a dog.

On the left, a cat is meowing; on the right, the cat is purring.

Now with your left eye look up toward your left brain. Move the eye so that it seems to circle in that space and explore it, let it roam all around. Do the same thing for a while with the closed right eye on the right side of the brain.

Try to circle vertically with the left eye anywhere you like so long as it is in the space of the left side of your head. You need not limit the circles to the brain space but do keep them inside the head. Then try to circle vertically on the right side, or imagine doing so, circling with your right eye.

Try to make some circles on the left side that tilt a little, with the left eye, of course. Try to circle at many different angles, making many overlapping circles. Do that for a while on the left side of the head; and then do it with the right eye on the right side.

Now with both eyes, circle vertically just in the middle of the head. You should circle along the corpus callosum, the ridge where the hemispheres of the brain come together. With both eyes together, circle as widely as you can inside your head.

Make some circles that go off to the left and some that angle off to the right. You may have to stop and start again very slowly in order to do this. Circle in one direction; and then stop and circle in another. Make a great many overlapping circles at different angles, as you did on the left and the right sides, but now fill the whole of your brain space and the inside of your head with them.

Stop and let your eyes come completely to rest. Try to make horizontal circles with both eyes just at the level of your eyes and circling as widely as possible inside your head.

Now try making smaller circles horizontally and at the level of your eyes. Make them smaller, and smaller, and smaller until you get down to a space that is too small for circling and then you will want to fix on that point and try to hold it. Do not hold your breath, or tense your muscles, or strain in any way. If you lose the point, then make more circles, making them smaller and smaller until you get back down to a point, then stay fixed on that point for as long as you can without much effort.

This, by the way, is an excellent meditation exercise when done by itself. Just make smaller and smaller circles, down to the point, and then remain fixed on that point for as long as possible, avoiding any strain as you do it.

Rest for a moment. Then, in the middle of your forehead, imagine the letter A, a big letter A. Then erase the A.

Simultaneously, imagine a letter A on the left and a number 2 on the right. Then erase them.

Imagine that there is a big 1 right in the middle of your forehead.

Let go of that, and imagine that there is an A on the left, and just a little to the right of the A, a 10.

Let them go, and imagine on the left a 1, and on the right an A, both of them there together at once. Let them go now, and imagine the A on the left and the 1 on the right.

Let them go, and imagine two ones (1 1) on the left, along with two A's (A A) on the right. Let them fade away. Breathe easily and if you need to adjust your position to be more comfortable, do so.

Now, in the middle of your forehead, see or imagine a triangle. Then imagine the triangle just inside the top of your head. Try to move it to the inside of the back of your head, so that if your eyes could turn completely around in your head, they would be looking at it.

Now raise the triangle up along the back of the head to the top and then on down to the forehead. Imagine it moving along the inside of the head from the forehead back to the top and then to the back of the head, and then to the top and back to the forehead. The triangle should make vertical semicircles on the inside of your skull.

Now just look at the triangle in front of you and imagine that it is not just a triangle but a pyramid. Beside the pyramid is a person riding on a camel. From what direction is that person riding? From the left, from the right, or from some other direction?

Take a little while, but not more than a minute, to stretch out on the floor or stand or do whatever you like. Give yourself a change of position. You may want to straighten your legs or flex your knees. Do whatever makes you comfortable, and then be seated once again.

Close your eyes and look up at your brain space. Imagine a sailboat moving on blue water and take note of how the sailboat moves.

Let that image fade away and imagine a car traveling on a highway. Observe the motion of the car.

Let that go, and imagine a man walking. Try to become more and more aware of him as he walks. He stops, then he walks some more, then he breaks into a run. He slows down and then he stops again.

Let the man go, and look for a car once again. Observe the car and watch it accelerate, then slow down and stop, then start up again, going faster and faster as it circles around the track which is the inside of your head.

Now the track is outside your head, and the car circles round and round you, moving like a halo whirling, or like the rings around a planet.

Imagine that there are many roads spiraling around

your head, and that the car starts at the top and goes round and round until it gets to your chin and then spirals back up until it gets to the top of your head; and let it stop there.

Now yawn and let the car drive down over your nose and into your mouth and swallow it and forget all about it.

Now focus your attention on your brain again and try to meditate on it. Concentrate on the left side of your brain for a while. Be aware that both of your eyes are looking in that direction but note that the sensation is better in the left eye. The sensation of looking is more clear.

Now look up at the right side of your brain and meditate on it. Hold it in your awareness and try to imagine what your brain looks like on the right side and on the left side. Think about your brain's convolutions, all those indentations on its surface. Think about the ridge that runs between the two hemispheres. Think about the gray matter of your brain.

Now try to sense both sides at once, the whole brain. Think of the skull and the inside of the skull, that brain with its changing electrical impulses and its changing chemistry. Meditate on it as the most complex single mechanism that exists in our world. Nothing we have built can rival it.

Just imagine for a moment that you can expand and contract your brain. Imagine that you can make it pulsate, and experience those pulsations for a while. As you hold the image of the brain, let it rest and, speaking directly to your brain, suggest to it that it will function better and better. Suggest that as time goes by more of its cells will be active and will function better.

Suggest that you will have more brain cells accessible to you and that the interaction of the cells and all the processes of the brain will continuously improve as time goes by.

It may be that, for the first time, you are talking directly to your own brain and that as you talk to it your brain is able to respond and give you what you are asking for. Tell yourself that it really can do that, and it *will* do that if you give it the attention the body craves.

Like the rest of the body, the brain does not want to be ignored. It will function better when it receives attention, and through the nervous system, will enhance the functioning of the entire body.

Now focus your attention one more time on the whole of the brain. Be aware of the space it occupies within the head. Try to sense that whole magnificent living structure which nature so prizes that it built a vault around it to guard it better than any other part of your body.

Now open your eyes and look around and observe. Are there any changes in your visual perceptions, whether of colors, forms, textures, or dimensionality? Observe whether you are sensing your head, and especially the back of your head, more clearly than usual. Is your head more clearly present in your body image now?

Note whether you feel relaxed and whether you can observe yourself closely enough to be able to say that your consciousness is altered and how it is altered.

Try to remember whether toward the end of the exercise the images were coming any more easily or quickly. Observe yourself closely and see whether you can discern any other effects of this exercise.

Slowly get up, stretch, and move around the room, suggesting to yourself as you do that you are becoming more and more wide awake.

Stimulating
the Nervous System

IN THIS EXERCISE, as in the preceding one, we will focus on the brain, but also experientially explore the brain's connections with other parts of the body through the nervous system. The lesson is not one in neuroanatomy or neurophysiology, and the sophisticated reader should not try to make a scientific critique on the basis of a literal understanding of the instructions given. He should, rather, suspend his judgment, which will only serve to block his experience or dilute it, and assume that it is a symbol system being worked with. Then he or she, like the reader who is unconcerned with evaluating each instruction for scientific accuracy, will find that experiences are being had which also will be very difficult to really explain from the scientific standpoint.

Seat yourself comfortably, close your eyes, and try to sense the interior of your mouth for a while. See if you can bring your tongue into your awareness, and your teeth, the roof and floor of your mouth, and that whole cavity there inside of your mouth.

See whether you can sense the interiors of the nasal passages. Breathe in and out, slowly or quickly, deeply or shallowly, continuously or in bursts, whatever is helpful to your sensing. Close first one nostril and then the other with a finger: It is easier for most people to sense the interior of the nose if they breathe in and out through just one nostril. Take your fingers away and breathe in and out through both nostrils, sensing what you are doing.

Now ignore the breathing and just try to sense the nasal cavities. Sense them as far back as you can, trying to follow the passageways beyond the nose.

Shift your attention to your eyes. Try to sense the outlines of your eyeballs, their weight, their surfaces, and try to sense as far back inside your head as you can everything that lies behind the eyes and is connected to them.

Sense or imagine you are sensing back behind the eyes and on into the brain, as far as you can go, as long as you still feel a connection to the eyes.

Now try to sense or imagine vividly where the brain is, whichever it seems to you that you can do. Explore the inside of the skull, the convoluted surface of the brain, the two hemispheres of the brain, the corpus callosum (the pathway between the two hemispheres).

Move your attention back along that pathway, down

to the brain stem and the base of the skull. Try to find the place where your spine connects with the brain stem, and then focus on the brain stem, the oldest part of the brain, or just imagine it. Keep your attention on the brain stem and suggest to yourself that you are getting into closer and closer contact with the ancient, primitive part of your brain.

Imagine and try to feel a connection between the base of the brain at the back and your eyes, as if a line is running from each eye to that part of the brain. As you breathe in and out, imagine that impulses are traveling back and forth between the brain stem and the eyes.

Then raise your attention a little higher, up to the space that is approximately behind your eyes, inside your head. And as you breathe in and out, imagine lines running back from the eyes through the head to the interior of the skull.

Raise your attention a little further, to about the height of the middle of your forehead, and imagine lines from the eyes moving up to that higher level of the brain, impulses traveling back and forth between that part of the brain and the eyes.

Then raise your attention to the top of the brain, the highest, newest region at the very top, just under the top of your skull. Think of the lines traveling from the eyes up toward that part of the brain. Let those lines go from the pupil of each eye to the center of the upper brain.

Now connect these three points in a triangle and use the brain to shape that triangle and send impulses through it, and let your eyes follow. Look over toward your right eye, then toward the top of your head (the apex of the triangle), back down to the left eye, and over to the right eye along the base.

Reverse the direction. Look from your right eye over to the left eye, then up to the apex and over to the right eye again, and keep tracing the triangle.

Now direct your attention to the left side of your brain. Look around, as it were, inside your head, all around on the left at first, sensing the ear and the passages of the ear coming into the head on the left side, the mouth, the ear passages, the nasal cavity, the eyes.

And then try to imagine the whole brain as clearly as you can. Think about the convolutions. Let your mind roam over the surface of the brain, traveling down along those convolutions and experiencing the brain as a living thing, as electrical, chemical, something incredibly complex, and constantly in motion.

Feel it as if it were contracting and expanding. Get a clearer and clearer sense of it, the brain inside your skull. And think of that brain responding now to the directions of your mind as you speak to it, telling it to come increasingly into your awareness, its outlines, its activities, the messages it sends and receives.

Now, while still concentrating on the brain, sense your right hand and, without moving it at all, imagine that your right hand is clenching into a fist. Imagine that signals are traveling down the right arm to the hand, instructing it to make a fist. See whether you can sense the right hand responding, ever so slightly, to these signals (even though you have not actually clenched your fist).

Now send the message that the hand is relaxing and

opening, and see if you sense any difference in the hand. Again send a message to the right hand to make a fist.

Keep the hand motionless but imagine strongly that you are making a fist and that you can feel the impulses traveling down to the hand and the hand beginning to make that fist, the muscles organizing as soon as the message is received.

And then imagine the hand opening and see if you can distinguish that slight change in the organization of the muscles as you withdraw the suggestion that the hand make a fist, and then do it once more.

Imagine strongly that the hand is going to make a fist, that the brain is sending messages telling the hand to do so, while something else tells the hand not to actually make the fist, but to respond only as it would to the suggestion that it make an imaginary fist.

And then suggest that the hand open, that it open widely and that it become very limp and relaxed . . . a message to the hand that it become very limp and relaxed.

Now concentrate on your brain and see whether your awareness is more on the right or the left side of the brain, the hand, the arm. See whether you're more aware now of your right side or your left, and then bring both sides of the brain equally into awareness.

Look over to the left with your eyes, feel the brain on the left side, imagine it, feel the whole brain inside the skull.

Now shift your awareness to the base of your spine, and up the spine through the brain stem, on up to the top of the brain, and back down again. Keep doing that, remembering to breathe freely while you do.

See if you are unusually aware of the spine in the area of the neck, the cervical vertebrae. Transfer your attention to the top of the brain, then down through the older parts of the brain, the brain stem, down the neck, down the back, all the way down to the coccyx, and then bring it back up again.

And as you go down to the base of the spine, see whether you have a clearer awareness of the rectum and genitals than you had before. Follow this awareness as it travels up and down the spine, from the top of the head down to the base of the spine. Imagine those impulses traveling all the way down to the genitals and then back up.

Sense the brain and the spine beneath it, the anus and the genitals, all the way from the top of the body down to the space between the legs and back up again, sending messages up and down the spine.

Now let the mind suggest to the brain and the nervous system that energy is gathering at a point near the base of the spine and the genitals, and that this energy will flow into the spine and up through the brain, all the way to the top of the head and then all the way back down again.

Energy flowing up and down through the spine. Bring it up to the brain and keep it there, and imagine it now swirling around inside your head.

Imagine it circling inside your skull, circling around through your brain and energizing the brain. Let your eyes feel that they can pivot back inside the head and sweep across the brain, vertically, horizontally, or obliquely.

Imagine that you're bringing the energy down to a point just above your nose and directly between the eyes, and that it's circling, circling there. And more energy is flowing up the spine to that spot between the eyes, going up there and circling, and circling and circling, and swirling, and then moving up to the top of the head, and swirling, and circling in a horizontal plane just beneath the top of the skull.

Use your eyes to watch it as it swirls, white energy, golden energy, circling around the top of the skull. Then start moving it down a little bit, making the circles bigger as the energy swirls around and around inside the forehead, down to the level of the eyes. Then swirling around the brain stem, the old brain stimulated, turned on by the swirling, the energy directed by the mind.

All you have to do to make changes in the brain is to imagine them happening, just as you can make changes in your hand simply by imagining them; these changes will occur whether you can sense them or not. Imagine this happening now, the energy intensifying and swirling around your brain, firing off neurons and stimulating the brain cells, the electrical activity, the chemical activity, making more brain cells alive and available.

Now you are more and more aware of what is happening inside your head, thinking that your brain is becoming more and more active, more and more stimulated, that you can become more and more aware, more and more alert, your brain is quicker, more agile, more intelligent.

And think of your brain as flooding the nervous system with messages, messages about better functioning, more accurate relays, more efficient circuitry, all the way down through the nervous system. The brain sending this stimulation, this tonic, a massage of the whole nervous system coming down from the brain.

Feel the energy flowing down the spine, through the torso and the genitals, the arms and legs, the hands and feet, intensifying as it flows through your body and as you become more keenly aware of your nervous system. You are sensing something now that many of you never have before, the nerves within your body.

You realize that something is happening inside your body; you can feel the flow of energy, the activity and the excitation of the nerves throughout the body, and the brain directing that flow of energy, vitality and awareness.

See if you can feel the energy in your spine now. Do you have a clearer image of the spine than you did before? Is it easier to imagine the vertebrae, the eyes and ears, nose and mouth, the inside of your skull, the nerves branching out from the spine to every part of your body? Can you imagine the brain transmitting its instructions everywhere, charging and renewing the body with new sensations of wholeness and vitality?

Breathe in a little more deeply, hold yourself a little more erect, and see if that increases the awareness of the internal flow through the nervous system. Now think for a moment of your skeleton, the muscles around the bones, the joints relaxing as the muscles let them go, the mind signaling the brain, the nervous system talking to the muscles, muscles freeing the skeleton, the whole body-mind working together as a unified whole.

Now once more return your awareness to the base of the spine. Think of energy concentrating there and rising up the spine and up into the head, surging up through the body into the brain, the body alive with energy, alive with the flow of energy, the whole nervous system active and alive.

Let the energy flow up from the body to the brain. Contract the rectum several times, see whether that helps the energy flow, brings the whole body even more to life. Contract the anus and the genitals. See if that further charges the nervous system, stimulates the energy flow.

Now just let it rise up to the brain and turn your attention there for a while as the energy of your entire body flows into your brain, and as all of the brain's functions are charged and heightened by this flow of new energy.

Let your attention linger in your brain for a little while and then slowly open your eyes, look around you, observe your perception of light, forms, and textures. Some of you will now be seeing much more, especially if the room is well lighted. Just observe how you feel now.

Lie down, stand, do whatever you like, but be quiet for a little while. Observe what you feel now.

Observe your hearing, your breathing. Do you feel

relaxed and energized at the same time? Walk around a little and see how you feel. Does your body feel different? And, if so, how? Sense your body image, your fingers particularly, how you move.

Sonic Vibrations in the Body (Part One)

LIKE THE BRAIN EXERCISE just completed, the following exercises will involve comparatively little bodily movement as we usually think of it. In fact, there will be continuous movement, but it will be inside of the body, not in space.

The next two exercises can be combined to intensify their physical, mental, and emotional effects. It is possible to do the first exercise by itself when time is limited. The second exercise, however, will be far more effective when it is preceded by the first.

One of the main effects of these exercises will be to bring more completely into awareness some parts and functions of the body of which we are usually barely, if at all, conscious—and thus to make the body image more complete. Most people will find that the exercises also produce a state of greater relaxation than other methods they have tried. Careful self-observation will reveal that this relaxation is physical, mental, and emotional. In the second part of the exercise, relaxation may come only after a temporary heightening of physical, mental, and emotional tension.

These exercises can result in profoundly altered states of consciousness if that is the intention. As with chemically-induced altered states, it may be necessary to experiment and learn how to allow the consciousness to alter, as well as how to make the best use of the states achieved. With such experimentation and learning, these exercises can be valuable aids in exploring realms of consciousness which are usually inaccessible. In those altered states it is also possible to give yourself therapeutic or otherwise beneficial suggestions which the body-mind will accept and act upon with an unusual facility and effectiveness.

In the following exercises the creation of sound and self-stimulation by sound will be used to bring about the desired effects. Sound directed both into one's own body and into the body of another person can have very powerful consequences. Many ancient psychophysical systems recognized this and developed a great variety of sounds and ways of generating sounds which became important techniques for growth, healing, and many other purposes. However, to use sound in those ways requires some guidance by a teacher. We give you here those experiences which it is safe and beneficial to have without such guidance.

The second part of the exercise should especially provide an aesthetically pleasing experience. The self-expression made possible can be both beautiful, profound, and self-revelatory, as well as emotionally cathartic. Musically oriented people may find in addition that they have discovered in themselves a new potential for creative work.

Assume a comfortable sitting position. And now make an *aah* sound. *aah*. Observe that to make the sound you have to open your mouth. *aaaaah*. Make the sound a number of times. Keep making the sound for at least 10 or 15 seconds in all cases. Now close your mouth but otherwise let the sound emerge just as before, whatever comes naturally so long as you keep in mind the *aah* sound you have been making. Observe that when the mouth is closed the *aah* necessarily sounds more like *mmmm*.

Keep your lips closed and clench your teeth and make the *mmmm* sound. Continue to make the *mmmm* sound. See whether it makes a difference if you open the teeth a little. Don't change anything else, just the teeth. *mmmm*. *mmmm*. Try it both ways, keeping the lips closed but clenching and unclenching the teeth.

Now make the *aah* sound with the mouth open and try to feel it up in your head where the brain is. *aah*. *aah*. *aah*. Try to project the sound up there. Try it with your eyes closed and your eyes open and see whether one way is better. *aah*. *aaah*. *aaaah*.

Now, as you continue to make that sound, plug your right ear, with your middle finger or by folding up your ear lobe (try it both ways). *aah. aah.* Notice carefully how you're hearing that. Then, keeping the right ear plugged, slap your thigh several times, loudly enough so that you can hear it plainly. *slap. slap.* Notice the difference in the ways that you hear those two sounds. Do it again, keeping the right ear plugged with the right middle finger: *aah. aah. slap. slap.* Continue with that a few more times.

Are you aware that when the noise is generated from within you, you feel that you hear it with the ear that is stopped up? And when the noise is generated outside you, as by that slapping, you hear it with the other ear, the ear that is not stopped up. If you didn't notice that before, do the same thing again with the ear stopped up and notice the difference. *aah. aah. slap. slap.*

Now stop up both of your ears and make the *aah* sound. *aah.* Do it with your mouth open. *aah.* Then do it with your mouth closed. *mmmm.* And then alternate opening and closing the mouth, so you get the two different sounds. *aah. mmmm. aah. mmmm.* Make it as loud as you can with the mouth open and with the mouth closed, and you will see that when the mouth is closed, the volume can be greatly increased, so that the whole head vibrates. You can achieve a much greater volume than when the mouth is open. Do it both ways several times. *aah. mmmm. aah. mmmm.*

You will see that the volume is related to how wide the mouth is open. As you open your mouth, the sound gets softer. As you close your mouth, the sound gets louder. Try that. *aah. mmmm. aah.* If you open your mouth as wide as possible—as though you were making

a very big yawn—the sound will almost fade away.
Continue with your hands resting on your legs.
Mouth open. *aah.* Mouth closed. *mmmm.* You can also
continue for a longer time as you wish. Continue: *aah.*
mmmm. aah. mmmm.

Use a finger to stop up your right nostril and continue, with your mouth closed. *mmmm.* See whether
now you seem to be hearing the sound mainly with
your left nostril instead of with your ear. *mmmm.* Your
strongest sense of sound is in the nostril that is not
stopped up.

Remember that if you stop up your ear, the sound is
greatest in the one that is stopped up. If you stop up
the nostril, you sense sound more strongly in the one
that is not stopped up. How would you explain that apparent inconsistency?

Now stop up both nostrils and try it. Alternately stop
up the left nostril and the right one. *aah. aah.* Close
your mouth and continue: *mmmm. mmmm.* You should
note that when you open the mouth, the sound will
seem to be in the mouth. When you close the mouth,
the sound will seem to be in the stopped-up nostril. Alternate opening and closing the mouth a few times.
aah. mmmm. aah. mmmm.

Now stop up both of your nostrils and make the
sound. *aaah.* If your mouth is completely closed, of
course you can't make a sound. Try opening the
mouth a little, then opening it wide, with both nostrils
blocked. *aaah.*

Observe that as the mouth closes you sense the
sound increasing in your nostrils. As the mouth opens,

you stop sensing the sound in your nostrils and begin to hear it inside your mouth. *aaah.* Now try stopping up both nostrils and both ears and try it, using your thumbs and middle fingers. *aaah.* When both ears and both nostrils are stopped up, you hear with the ears, or so it seems. *aaah.*

Keeping your ears plugged, release the nostrils and try it several times: *aaah.* You see, you continue to hear with the ears so long as they are stopped up.

So the human head is a rather curious acoustical chamber. If you stop up an ear, you hear with that ear so long as the noise comes from within. If it comes from without, you hear with the ear that is not stopped up. Try to remember the other variations we have explored. There are many more as yet unexplored.

Now, once again, stop up the ears and make the sound, first with the mouth open—*aah*—and then with the mouth closed—*mmmm. aah. mmmm. aah.* Think about the famous Indian chant word *aum.* Pronounce it *aah oom, aah oom,* as two separate syllables. Say it a few times, opening the mouth for the *aah* and closing it for the *oom* and keeping the ears stopped. *aah. oom. aah. oom. aah. oom. aaah. ooom.*

Make the whole inside of your head really vibrate with that sound. Amplify the sound, so that the whole inside of the head becomes filled with it: *aah. oom.*

Try directing the sound to the right side of the brain. *aah. oom.* Fill the whole right side of your head with sound. It is probably better for the present to do it with the eyes closed. Continue to vibrate the entire right side of your brain. *aah. oom. aah. oom. aah. oom.*

Stop a moment, and see whether you feel any difference between the right side of the face and the left, the right eye and the left eye, the right temple and the left one.

Now, with the ears stopped up, project the *aah oom* up to the left side of the brain. Fill the left side of the head from about the cheekbone up with powerful vibratory sound. *aah. oom. aah. oom. aah. oom.* See how long you can extend the duration of the *oom* sound. *aah. oooommmmmmmm.*

Now, with the ears blocked, try filling the whole head at once, from about the cheekbone up, with the *aah oom. aah. oom.* Try to make the *aah* vibrate as powerfully as the *oom. aah. oom. aah. oom. aah. oom.* To amplify the *aah,* block the nostrils as well as the ears, releasing them to make the *oom* sound. Block them to make the *aah* and then release them to make the *oom,* always directing the sounds up into the head. *aah. oom.* Now see whether you can get the *aah* to vibrate up there without blocking the nostrils. *aah. oom. aah. oom.*

Now rest for a moment and just experience the sensations created by what you have been doing. Lie down and observe how you feel. As you lie there make a humming sound, *mmmm,* in your head and direct that sound upward toward the top of your head. Don't do anything with your hands, just direct the sound upward as you lie on your back. *mmmm.*

See whether you can send that sound in the direction of your right eye and temple for a while. *mmmm.* Now send it toward the left eye and temple. *mmmm.* Then try to fill the whole head again. *mmmm.*

Now try to do it in a higher tone. Raise your voice a little and do it. Try it with your fingers in your ears. *mmmm.* Then sit up and do it. *mmmm.* Keep trying to raise the sound higher while stopping up the ears. *mmmm.*

Now make the sound you have made from the beginning, the lower sound, and direct it toward the base of your skull, toward the old brain—the brain stem—and the top of the spine. *mmmm.* Direct it a little higher, toward the back of your skull. Try to fill the inside of the back of your head with sound. *mmmm.* Bring it forward to the area inside the forehead and to the eyes. Make the sound vibrate with your ears stopped. *mmmmmm.*

Now try to focus that sound, sending it to a spot between the eyes, just a little above the bridge of the nose. That is the location of the so-called third eye, one of the yoga chakras. This is also the site of the pineal gland, an important gland that many have felt is intimately bound up with any kind of extrasensory perception or paranormal capacity.

Now, with your ears stopped, try to bombard your "third eye" with sound vibrations. You can do it in different ways, making the *mmmm* higher or lower, or introducing a kind of quaver into it, breaks in the continuity, so that it becomes almost a buzz.

Direct all these sounds to the "third eye," concentrating them there as intensely as possible. *mmmm. mmmm.* Make explosions of sound— *m m m*—and try to feel the sound as though it were hammering against the inside of your forehead and that third-eye area. *m m m m.*

Imagine that you are pounding it with sound vibrations, stimulating it, trying, gradually, to break through an obstruction that is blocking it, to open it up. Keep hammering away at it but not too hard. *mm mm mm mm mm.*

Now bombard it with steady sound. Then stimulate it with discontinuous sounds. Do it one way for a while, then the other way. *mmmm mm mm mm mmmm.*

Now direct these sounds to the very top of your head. This is the location of another yoga chakra called the thousand-petal lotus. It is also the newest area of the brain, an area which has potential we have not yet tapped. It is said that were we able to realize this potential in our everyday lives we would be truly aware and awake, more completely conscious than we have ever been before.

Now flood that area with sound. All kinds of sound, steady and intermittent, high and low. Vibrate it, stimulate it as powerfully as you can. *mmmmmmmmm mm mm mm m m m m mm mmmmmmmmmm.*

Make columns of sound rising up to the very top of your brain, stimulating it. *mmmmmmmmm mm mm mm m m m m mm mmmmmmmmmm.*

For a moment, direct the sound toward the "third eye," then toward the brain near the base of the skull, then toward the top again. Now fill the entire head with sound vibrations. *mmmmm mm mm mm m m m mmmmm mm m mm.*

Flood the brain with giant *aums.* Flood the whole brain. *aah oom. aah oom. aah ooomm. aah oooomm.* Do it as powerfully as you are able to. Give yourself up completely to the vibrations in your head.

What, if anything, has changed? Try to observe your movements, your muscles, your joints, your breathing, how you sense your face and your head. How do you feel mentally and emotionally? Compare your state of consciousness now with your state of consciousness at the start of the exercise.

Lie down a moment and note how the body lies on the floor. Observe your body image and again try to observe as closely as possible your own consciousness. Do you feel relaxed?

Then get up slowly and walk around and note how you hold yourself when you walk. Remember to observe as much as you can—the weight of the head, the sensations in the head and neck. Stay silent for a while and continue to increase your self-awareness—physical, mental, emotional.

As mentioned at the outset, you can either stop when this exercise is completed or, after a short rest, begin the next one.

Sonic Vibrations (Part Two): Song of the Self

WE HAVE ALREADY STATED that you perform this exercise immediately after Part One, since your present state of awareness will be of considerable help in realizing the effects of Part Two. These effects will be more psychological and emotional than those of the earlier exercises, though they will still contribute to your growing internal awareness and to the completion of your body image. Try to observe any changes of consciousness that accompany this exercise.

Sit down in a comfortable position, a yoga-type position if you can.

Close your eyes and try to become conscious of the outside of your head. This means the face, top and back of the head, underside of the chin, and the neck right down to where the shoulders begin. Be particularly aware of the eyes, the cavity behind the eyes; the ears, ear cavity; mouth, mouth cavity; nose, nose cavity. Go over them one by one. Sense those cavities as fully and as far back as you can. Try to follow the mouth on down the throat, right on through the intestines. And, if you like, let that awareness just come on down through the other end.

Now try to be aware of your brain and follow it on down the spinal cord. Let your awareness go on down the spinal cord to the end. And then come back up to the brain stem. Try to do that as methodically as possible, several times.

While you are doing this, put your middle fingers in your ears and fill the brain area with the *aah oom* sound that is now familiar to you. Now just close your eyes. Keep making those sounds for a couple of minutes while you scan your brain and then try to follow the spinal cord down to the coccyx, or tailbone, and then come all the way back up.

Now, try to perceive the skeleton in its entirety. Perhaps that will make it easier to bring the vertebrae into your awareness. Begin with the skull: the top and sides, the eye sockets, and the jawbones. Be aware of the neck, shoulder bones, ribs, front and back, and the bones in the upper arms, forearms, hands, pelvis, upper legs, lower legs, feet, and toes. Be aware of the joints in the ankles, knees, toes, fingers, wrists, elbows, shoulders, and the articulations of the spine. With the spine, begin at the neck; that may be the easiest to be aware of. Try moving the head a little bit.

Continue making the *aah oom* sound, flooding your brain with it, and become as aware as you can of the whole skeleton, beginning with the skull. Try to imagine yourself as just a skeleton sitting there as you make that sound in your brain cage. Withdraw your awareness from the other parts of your body, muscles and flesh, and think of yourself as just a skeleton sitting there in a room with other skeletons or by yourself. Just a skeleton sitting there in whatever position you are sitting in, that sound resounding in your head, filling the inside of the skull, continuing through eternity, a timeless moment, a little eternity.

Lie down and make the *aah oom* sound, continuing to be aware of the skeleton, the skeleton lying on the floor. See whether that is easier. Experiment with different sounds, higher, lower, discontinuous. Try to move the sound through different parts of the skeleton. See if you can vibrate the whole skeletal structure.

Now consider that the rest of your body is coming into being, that flesh is beginning to cover the skeleton. Everywhere within that covering are veins, arteries, blood, and nerves. And imagine that the sonic vibrations are going to bring the body to life, to awaken all the functions of the body.

And as you lie there, become more and more aware of the whole body around that skeleton and of the stimulation by the sonic vibrations of the whole body. Feel the vibrations going through the nerves, through the muscles and the flesh, the whole body brought to life by the vibrations.

Now sit up again, eyes closed, and try to direct the

vibrations toward the top of the head, the very top. Plug up your ears and do that.

Experiment with different sounds to see what you find most stimulating. Is it high sounds, low sounds, discontinuous sounds, buzzing sounds? What sounds have the greatest impact on you? Direct the sounds to the top of your skull. Try to find sounds that are pure. Imagine a column of pure sound and light rising up through the center of your brain and passing through the top of the skull, higher and higher. Do that now.

Now let the column of sound grow larger so that it fills the entire head and extends beyond it like a great vibration of sound and light penetrating far into space, like a great beacon.

Imagine that you can project that beacon far into space. You can focus it on different stars, aim it at any intelligent life that you feel might be there. You can imagine if you will, believe if you will, that it is a kind of prayer, that you are reaching out to the Highest Power with that beacon. Pure sounds, vibratory sounds, whatever you feel is appropriate and effective.

Now try to transform your humming into music. Project music through the entire brain. Create the music of the spheres, or a message that you want to send. But make music and fill your whole head with it. Ears stopped up, eyes closed: Create music.

And now keep the music inside your head and sing to your brain. Sing to your brain and, without using words, sing the song of your existence, of your life up to now, of your hopes for the future. Sing to your brain and the different levels of your psyche. This is a song to the brain, but also to the unconscious mind, a song to yourself that describes your past, your present, and what you want your future to be. Create that song now and flood the inside of your head with that music, the song of yourself. Plug up your ears and do it now.

Stop for a moment. Remember that whatever your brain can organize, you can do, within human limits. The brain and the mind together constitute your reality, have access to your potential, and so now you hymn yourself. Sing the song of yourself, that humming that you flood your brain with, the message of what you want your life to be, what you truly want. And convey that to your brain, your mind, your brain-mind. Let it rise from your depths, convey it passionately, as beautifully as you can. Just flood the brain with that music, that message. You may be surprised at the song that comes and what you learn about yourself.

Stop. Sit silently for a moment. Your attention is still focused on your brain. The brain is assimilating that message and the message is programming the brain for your future. Leave it to your brain for a moment to integrate and begin the reorganization necessary to carry out the program that you have given it.

Pay no attention to the images you may be receiving. Some people will have negative, even demonic, images at this point. This means that some negative aspects of yourself are being reprogrammed. Now, flood your brain with sound again to give it further energy to free itself of negative programs. Exorcise yourself with pure sound now for a while. Flood your brain-mind with sound to facilitate the reorganization of yourself that you have begun. Do it now, a chant of exorcism and banishment. Flood the brain.

Continue now to purge yourself, to purify yourself with the vibration of sound flooding your brain and reaching the deepest levels of your mind. Do it powerfully, intensely, feel the sound resounding throughout the brain, filling the skull, bringing light and change. Do it now.

Now, finally imagine that you are seated on a mountaintop or a hilltop beside the sea and that it is dawn. A new day is coming. The sun is bringing up a new future, a new day. And this time fill your brain with a hymn to that new dawn, a greeting to that new beginning. A Song to the Dawn. Do it now.

Stop. Sit or lie quietly for a few minutes and just see how you feel. Don't analyze, just feel. Then you can walk around if you like. Observe yourself—your emotions, sensations, perceptions. Quietly allow yourself to integrate what you have experienced.

Using Words and Images to Alter the Body

IN THE CHAPTER called "The Mind, the Brain, and the Body," we discussed various ways in which verbal instructions and images are used to effect both minor and profound changes in the human body. Words and images have the same power in everyday life, although we are rarely conscious of how we are affected by them. We will now give you a practical demonstration and let you observe this power for yourself.[1]

---

[1] Our book *Mind Games: The Guide to Inner Space* (New York: Delta Books, 1973) also experientially demonstrates induced changes in the body and the body image. It has a very different approach from the present volume and is more mind-oriented, but it also contains a systematic method for evoking latent human potentials so that groups could very fruitfully use the two books together.

First lie on your back and scan your body image. Observe where it is clear, where it is faint, and where there are gaps or unsensed areas. As we work, the body and the body image will change, quite recognizably.

Lie with your arms at your sides, palms down, and go over your body once again. Be aware of how your feet are lying, your lower legs, your knees, your upper legs, your pelvis, buttocks, abdomen, hands, forearms, elbows, upper arms, shoulders, chest, back, neck, face, eyes, forehead, mouth, the back of your head. And be sure that you are breathing normally.

Now focus on your left foot and just flex the toes of the left foot a few times. Note the sensations carefully and then imagine as vividly as you can that you are flexing them, ten or fifteen times, while continuing to breathe normally. Now actually flex the foot four or five times—that is, bend and extend it at the ankle. Then imagine flexing the foot ten or fifteen times.

Bend your left knee slightly so that the back of the knee comes off the floor a little, and then let it fall lightly against the floor. Do it several times. Now imagine doing it ten or fifteen times. Then actually raise and gently drop the left knee ten or fifteen times, noting the sensation in the knee and the hip joint, the back of the foot and the heel. Now imagine doing it, and make sure that you include all those sensations and any others of which you were aware.

Rap five times with the palm of your left hand on the floor, just bending the hand at the wrist and leaving the forearm on the floor. Imagine doing it, recalling very vividly the sensations in the wrist and in the hand as it makes contact with the floor. Actually rap with the hand several times, but this time bend the arm at the elbow, so that the forearm comes off the floor. Then imagine doing it fifteen or twenty times.

Now rap again with the hand on the floor, but this time with the whole left arm extended, so that the movement is in the shoulder joint. As you raise the arm and lower it, note the sensations in the shoulder and the arm and how the hand makes contact with the floor when you rap. Note how the left side feels, and the rib cage. Now imagine making that same movement fifteen times.

With the palm of your left hand, stroke the left side of your face. Just rub the left hand up and down the face a few times, noticing both what the face feels and what the hand feels. Stroke the whole side of the face and head. Then put your hand back down at your side and imagine doing the same thing: stroking the face and remembering the sensations in the face and in the hand. See whether you recall the sensations in the shoulder when you were stroking your face.

Next, in your imagination only, move your left hand up and down the front of your body on the left side from the top of the chest to the pelvis and then on down the left leg. If you think it will be helpful, make several actual movements, then work again with your imagination. Try to sense clearly your body being stroked by your hand.

And then imagine that your left leg is being stroked by someone else's hand. The hand moves up and down the left leg, from the ankle to the top of the thigh. Then imagine two hands rubbing up and down your leg, one hand more to the outside of the leg and one more to the inside. You can think of a particular person, or the hands can just be anonymous.

Now imagine the bottom of your left foot being gently stroked and then stimulated by gently scratching fingernails. Then imagine that one hand takes hold of your foot and the other takes hold of each of your toes successively, pulling them, moving them back and forth. A finger rubs back and forth between the big toe and the second toe; then rubs between the next two toes, and so on. After it reaches the little toe, it comes back in the other direction, rubbing between each of the toes until it gets to the big toe again.

Now imagine that your masseur or masseuse, as you prefer, has a brush and is beginning to brush the bottom of your left foot (remember all instructions apply to the left side of your body). Feel the bristles of the brush on the bottom of your foot, a gentle but stimulating brushing, and then the brush working on the sides of your foot, and on the top. And then coming up your left side, massaging your leg wherever the brush can reach. Imagine it brushing the calf and the knee and the thigh, on the top and at the sides. If you have not given an identity to the person doing the massage, then don't do so now. Later you may be surprised to discover who it is.

Feel the brush moving up over your hip joint, brushing the entire left side of your body, the whole area to the left of your navel. The brush moves over the ab-

domen and chest, the fingers and hand and arm, over
the left shoulder and the neck. Then the brush makes
gentle contact with the left side of your face, your ear,
and the side of your head.

Rest a moment and observe how you are lying. Compare how the left side is lying with how the right side is
lying. See whether you are equally aware of them or
whether one side is clearer. Is there more sensation on
one side than on the other? Briefly open your eyes and
see whether you are looking to the left side, to the
right, or straight up. Look straight up and notice
whether your head inclines to one side. If it does, you
will feel a slight strain in the eyes when you look
straight up. Move your head so that your eyes can look
straight up without straining and then close your eyes
again.

Bend your left leg so that your foot is resting flat
on the floor and the top of the knee is pointing to
the ceiling, and sense the bottom of the foot against the
floor. Sense the toes as best you can, the top of the
foot, the lower leg, the knee, the upper leg, the hip
joint, the pelvis and abdomen on the left side, the left
buttock, the left breast, the left fingers and hand, the
left forearm, elbow, and shoulder. Sense the left side
of your mouth, your left cheek, the left side of your
forehead, and your left eye. Does it feel as though the
eye is looking straight up, or is it looking somewhat to
the side? Does the head lie straight, or does it tilt a little
to the left? If so, when did it move to the left? Try to
sense your head clearly and arrange yourself so that
the head and the eyes point straight up. Don't open
your eyes to do it, just use your sensing.

Rap several times with the bottom of your left foot on the floor, and then imagine doing it a few times. Rap with the left hand a few times, bending your arm at the elbow. Then imagine rapping with your left hand, bending at the wrist, then at the elbow, then lifting the whole arm. Put your leg down on the floor, extended.

Now your masseuse or masseur is going to work on you again, this time with oil. Imagine that first the foot is massaged, the warm oil being rubbed between the toes, then on the bottom of the foot, as the hands knead it gently, then on the top of the foot and the sides. Then the entire leg is oiled, the hands moving up the leg at a leisurely pace, rubbing the ankle, the calf, the knee, the thigh, massaging the oil into the leg. The hands pick up the leg, to work on the back of the leg, the calf, the back of the knee, and the thigh.

Then the left hip is massaged, and the buttock, the front of your body as far as the navel. It is a gentle, skillful massage of your abdomen, your entire upper body on the left side, including each finger, the hand and the arm, and the shoulder. Then the hands rub the oil into your neck and the left side of your face.

Next, hot, wet towels are applied to your left side, beginning with the face and the head, and working this time from the top of your body down. Give yourself plenty of time to imagine the entire process vividly, on down to your toes. Then the left side of your body is dried off with a towel, starting at the feet and working up to the head, briskly but thoroughly.

Then, finally, the hands go along your body, still on the left side, stimulating it with little slaps, both hands whacking you gently, just pleasant little slaps, starting at the bottoms of the feet and continuing on up to the shoulder. Then the hands rap very lightly with just the fingertips on your neck and face.

Rest a while and, as you lie there, breathe easily and observe carefully the two sides of your body. Note where your eyes are looking, and whether the head is turned. Observe whether there is any strain when you try to look straight up with your closed eyes.

Focus your attention on your left foot and leg. Now suggest to yourself ten times that the leg feels heavy and warm, that the blood is flowing through the left leg into the foot, and that the left leg feels comfortably heavy. Then suggest to yourself a few times that blood is flowing to the pelvis and the buttocks on the left side. Suggest that the blood is flowing into the left arm and hand and into the upper body on the left. Then suggest that the blood is flowing to the left side of your face, to your cheek, your head, your left eye. And repeat to yourself about ten times: *My left side is heavy, warm, and relaxed; my left side is heavy, warm, and relaxed.*

Now suggest to yourself that your left foot is feeling increasingly alive and coming increasingly into your awareness. As you suggest that a number of times, form a picture of the foot based on your sensing, using your imagination to fill in any gaps. Picture the left foot, its form and its surface, and suggest that it is getting easier to sense. Be aware of your toes, your heel, your whole foot, and sense how your left leg rests on the floor. Sense all around the lower leg, and then the upper leg, and then the entire leg. Sense and picture

the left side of the pelvis, the buttock, the hip, then the
left side of the abdomen. Then sense vividly and picture the left fingers, the hand, the arm, on up to the
shoulder. The upper body, the chest, the neck, the
mouth, the side of the face, and the eye, all, of course,
on the left side. Open your eyes and notice where you
are looking and whether the head is turned. Move the
head so that you are looking straight up. Close your
eyes again and sense your head on the left side.

Now imagine that a line runs down the middle of
your body, dividing the body all the way from the top
of the head to the crotch. Sense the whole left side and
imagine how it looks. Imagine flexing your left toes,
and then your left foot and ankle. Do it a number of
times. Then imagine bending your knee just a little,
and rapping with the back of the knee on the floor.
Imagine rapping your hand on the floor, bending your
arm at the elbow. Imagine the sensations in the hand,
the forearm, the elbow. Then sense the shoulder
movement as you imagine lifting the entire left arm to
rap on the floor. Sense and picture the entire arm as
you do that.

Now imagine simultaneously flexing the foot and
rapping on the floor with the palm, the arm bending at
the wrist. It is a simultaneous movement of the ankle
and wrist joints. Then flex just the toes and the fingers
simultaneously. Imagine alternately flexing the toes
and the fingers. Be sure you breathe normally as you
imagine these movements.

Quickly open your eyes one last time and notice
where you are looking. Direct the eyes so that they are

looking straight up and keep them there a while. If
there is any feeling of strain, move the head so that the
eyes are comfortable. Notice how much you have to
move your head this time. Again, did you notice when
your head turned, or your eyes, or was the movement
quite unconscious? Think about how many other unconscious movements you make when thinking, when
imagining, and in all kinds of situations.

Observe your body image for a moment. Compare
how you are lying on the left side with how you are
lying on the right side, and the clarity of the body
image on the two sides. When you have made a thorough comparison, roll slowly to one side and get up.
Move around a bit, again comparing your two sides.

Changing the Body
With Emotion

As WE HAVE SEEN FROM SOME of the preceding exercises, especially the last, it is quite possible to produce profound changes in the body through both words and sensory images. It is also possible to work specifically with the emotions to alter the body, although as far as we know such procedures have never been systematically employed in the past. (We exclude "pleasant images" to aid relaxation.)

It seems curious that no one has developed such a method. In everyday life, our emotions frequently cause alterations in the body which we are aware of—for example, the changes in the body which accompany such emotions as joy, fear, and desire. In the long run, inhibiting the expression of emotions takes a grim toll on the body. We need only to harness productively the body's learned and inherited abilities to change in response to different emotional states.

Much that happens in the body is clearly a product of emotions which are more or less unconscious, and which are themselves conditioned by attitudes which may be unconscious as well and even directly at odds with one's conscious beliefs. The profound influence of such unconscious or masked emotions on the state of the body may be the single most important determinant of our health, of much of our behavior, and indeed the whole course of our lives.

Of particular interest is the blunting and distortion of sensory experience by our conscious and unconscious attitudes. During our many years of research with psychedelic drugs and hypnosis we have found repeatedly that in a sufficiently altered state of consciousness, many people spontaneously recognize that their sensory experience is ordinarily distorted by ideas and values imposed upon them in childhood. The most common of these is a negative attitude toward matter itself and, by extension, toward the body. The invidious comparison of matter with spirit and thus of body with mind is evidently still implicit in our culture. These negative feelings dilute or blunt the body's experience of both itself and the world. It appears to be the sense of touch and perhaps the kinesthetic sense that suffer most from this deep-rooted conditioning. It is possible to overcome this conditioning, indeed it is essential if the health and well-being of the body are not to be continually eroded by this dosage of alienation and self-hatred administered early in life.

One basic and necessary change is to reorient the body toward pleasure. As we have said before, the nervous system is hedonistic by nature. We see the proof of this in the body's ability to change in countless ways once we have brought pleasurable new ways of being and functioning sufficiently into our awareness. The body is certainly rational enough to prefer pleasure to pain, but because of the early conditioning, the body's *right* to pleasure must be sanctioned and reaffirmed, in most cases, repeatedly. Of course, we are not speaking now of the infantile pleasure-seeking which can become a compulsion. But at work or play, or in any other pursuit, our use of our bodies should be light, easy, efficient, and pleasurable. The body reoriented toward pleasure and provided with pleasurable experiences will be healthier and the whole being will be the better for it.

There is a simple experiment we do with hypnotic subjects which immediately demonstrates the responses the body will make when reoriented toward pleasure. Without hypnosis, many people can experience the changes that occur. You have already achieved a greater than average sensitivity and awareness and will probably profit from this experiment.

Seat yourself comfortably on the floor, or in a chair if you prefer, and place both of your hands palms downward on your thighs. Focus your attention on your right hand and move it up and down your thigh, noting the sensations in both the hand and thigh. Now suggest to yourself many times that your right hand is becoming more and more sensitive, taking in more and more information, able to feel more completely. Keep moving the hand up and down the thigh, suggesting that it is becoming more sensitive, so that the thigh responds to the hand's heightened sensitivity. After a while, compare the sensations in the hand and in the thigh with those you experienced at first.

Compare the right hand now with the left one. Compare your awareness of your right hand and the thigh beneath the hand with your awareness of your left hand and left thigh.

Instruct your right hand to remain sensitized and then turn your attention to your left hand. Repeatedly suggest to your left hand that it is highly oriented toward pleasure—it is a pleasure-seeking hand, a hand that greatly enjoys and has every right to enjoy giving and taking pleasure. Continue with those suggestions as you move the left hand repeatedly up and down the left thigh. Think of the hand as receiving pleasurable sensations through touching, and as giving pleasure as it touches. Suggest that this pleasure can become more and more intense, and that it is a very good thing. Experience all the pleasure that the hand can provide. Keep moving it, be aware of what the hand is sensing and of what the thigh feels. Note whether the left hand moves and touches somewhat differently than the right hand did.

Stop now and compare the pleasure-seeking, pleasure-taking hand with the still-sensitized right hand. You have oriented your left hand toward pleasure and you have made your right hand as sensitive as possible. Note which hand feels more. Rub the left hand up and down the left thigh a few times and then rub the right hand up and down the right thigh. Based on the experience of the two thighs, which hand would you rather be touched by? It is usually the case that the greater the pleasure the body experiences, the greater the pleasure it is able to give. This is true whether you touch your own body or someone else's. We have often noticed that animals can obviously feel the difference between the touch of a hand that is oriented toward pleasure and one that is in its ordinary state, or even one that has been sensitized by suggestion.

Whether or not your experience fits this description, the following exercise should demonstrate clearly to you how feeings alter the body. The exercise can be done by one person, but it is especially interesting when done by a couple or a group.

To begin with, lie on your back and scan your body for a while. Note how it lies and examine your body image.

Rub the palms of your hands together. Which hand are you now more aware of? To equalize your awareness, clasp your hands together and interlace the fingers. Think of the pleasure orientation flowing from the left hand into the right, and of the increased sensitivity flowing from the right hand into the left one. Note whether your right thumb or your left thumb is on the outside when your hands are clasped. Unclasp the hands and clasp them again, putting the other thumb outside. Clasp and unclasp them a number of times, with first one thumb on the outside, then the other. Also interlace your fingers with the backs of the hands facing, and once again alternate the position of the thumbs. Clasp the hands with the two palms together and move the hands so that they make a clapping sound. Then put your hands and arms down at your sides, palms on the floor.

Now, with eyes closed, focus your awareness on your right hand. Try to sense clearly and picture your right little finger, then the ring finger, and so on to the thumb. You can move each finger several times if that makes the sensing clearer. Then bring all the fingers and the entire hand and wrist into your awareness. Be aware of both the top and the underside of the right hand as it rests on the floor. Focus as much of your attention on your right hand as possible. You must minimize your awareness of the other parts of your body as you become aware of your hand alone.

Think of your consciousness as being in your right hand. Try to imagine that you *exist* in your right hand. And recall some very pleasant experience as vividly as you can. You might think, for example, of how you felt when you were a child on Christmas morning and were just going into the room to find your presents under the Christmas tree. Your consciousness is now in your hand, and your hand is filling with the recollected emotion of that experience. Let your right hand be very, very light and joyous, filling up with the emotions that you are now recalling. Concentrate on this for a while.

Move your right hand along the floor, sensing the hand as you move it. Imagine and feel that hand to be light and bubbly—a hand that, if it could, would laugh with joy.

For a moment compare how the right hand feels with the feelings in the rest of the body. Does it begin to feel lighter and freer? What do you notice? Again, be conscious just of your right hand, give it your full attention, and again let it fill with emotion.

Let the happy, light, joyous feelings remain in the hand, but shift your awareness down to your right foot, and imagine those same feelings moving into your right foot. Be sure there is plenty to go around. More and more, be aware of the lightness and joyousness in your right foot. If it helps, you can wiggle your toes a little. Experience your right foot playfully and joyfully.

Experience the feelings of joy in the right hand and the right foot simultaneously. Add a few pleasant sensations, so that the toes can feel warm sand, and then try some nice warm mud. Let the joyous right hand and the joyous right foot feel the sun and the wind. Think about someone whose toes you would like to play with. Your toes and other toes playing together. Now think about that happy foot playing the piano—thumping away merrily. Think about doodling or drawing a picture with the toes of the right foot. (You can move the foot and toes if you like.)

Put the foot down if you have raised it. Now compare the joyous right foot and right hand with the other foot and hand. What differences do you notice? Observe whether the right foot and hand now feel lighter and much more alive. Compare the two sides of your body.

Get up and walk around a bit. Turn to the right several times as you walk, and several times to the left. Then lie down again. Ask yourself: Is to be more conscious to be more alive? Think about that for a moment, making sure that you do not hold your breath while you are thinking or tense the muscles in your face or anywhere else in your body.

Now, allow the good feelings to move through your leg, up to your knee while continuing to feel that joyousness in your right hand and foot. Let the happiness suffuse the leg and the knee and move your leg a little. Bend the knee a bit, the ankle, the toes, whatever it occurs to you to do. As you are doing that, note for a moment how the other knee feels and whether the difference between the two sides of the body is increasing. Notice whether the left leg now feels rather lifeless by comparison, and ask yourself whether that comparative lifelessness is not your normal state. Do you ordinarily feel somewhat lifeless? Which side feels heavier? And note whether one side feels shorter.

Stop moving your right leg and let the emotion flow again. This time, the joyous emotion and warmth are moving up the right forearm as far as the elbow. Make some small movements with your right hand and forearm and experience the joyousness and lightness of the movements.

At the same time, move the lower right leg and the lower right arm. How do they feel as compared to the left side?

Stop moving once again. Extend the warmth and good feelings on up through the upper leg and hip on the right side. Be aware of the good feeling and of an attitude of lovingness toward your own body. Add to that serenity: the feet, the calves, the upper leg, the hip, the right hand and lower arm, all serene.

Now be aware of the feelings flowing on through the entire right arm and shoulder. Feel that joyous delight flowing all the way up from the foot through the leg and from the fingertips on up through the shoulder. Move the right arm and the leg around a little—moving joyously and experiencing those good feelings with real pleasure.

Let the right arm and leg lie still. Extend the joyous feeling to the right buttock. Feel it to be a very happy buttock—a joyous and bubbly buttock.

Now let the right side of the pelvis join in, and the right side of the abdomen. If you want to move a little to increase these feelings, or savor them, then go ahead. But only move the happy right side.

Stop moving once again. Imagine that a line divides the two sides of your body, running from the top of your head down to your feet. Now extend the joyousness and the warmth and the happy feelings all through the right side of your body. Let the feelings flow, stream, however they move in your body. Feel the joy and the delight suffusing your right side, traveling on up through your chest, your neck, your face and head. Let the right side move as much as you like. You can make sensuous, sinuous, undulating movements, but only on that side. To further increase the joy and warmth and good feeling, make some movements with all the parts of your body that have been suffused with emotion up to now.

Stop moving once again. Compare the right side of your body up to the neck with the other side of your body. And also compare the two sides of your face. Be especially aware of the joyous, happy feelings on the right side of your face, and throughout your whole right side as well. Now just observe yourself and note whether perhaps the right side of your face is starting to smile while the other side remains expressionless.

Also as you feel the joyousness suffusing your entire right side, note what you are doing with your eyes. You are probably looking to the right where all the fun is, because there is much less to interest you on the left side. With some people there will now be a tendency for the whole face to try to move toward the right. The jaw, the mouth, and even the tongue may be trying to move toward the pleasure.

Note whether you are now breathing differently through the right nostril than you are through the left one, and whether when you pay attention to your breathing you notice a difference in your chest on the right side.

Try to become aware now of the entire right side of your body. Experience the whole body image on the right side, including the feelings and emotions. Try to move the whole right side of your body, from the tips of your toes to the top of your head. Move the right side any way you like and enjoy the feelings as you move.

Now try moving the whole body, both sides at once. Observe whether the body image is now clearer on one side than it is on the other, and whether you have a quite different sense of your body on the right side than the left. What do you notice? For example, does one side feel lighter and one side heavier? Observe whether one side feels longer and the other side shorter. Which side has greater freedom of movement? Which side feels awkward, clumsy, not very good or healthy by comparison? Move around some more and make comparisons.

Slowly get up and walk around. Note whether the sensations are more pleasant on one side than on the other. What else do you notice?

Now, if you have done this exercise with another person, move closer until your right sides are touching as completely and as closely as possible. Note how this feels, and turn around so that your left sides are touching. Note again how that feels.

Now stand with your right side touching your partner's left; then change positions, your left side touching your partner's right. Be as aware as possible of all of your feelings and sensations as you stand in different positions. Once again, stand with your right sides touching and enjoy the sensation. Do not bring your left sides together again, but go back to your original places and lie down again.

Since we have done nothing to change it, you have presumably been experiencing your left side as it is normally. However, you have been experiencing it in relation to your potential for being much happier and more alive than you usually are. Consider and compare that normal mode of being with your potential. If the revelation is in some respects unpleasant, it should also be hopeful. Your ability to change has been demonstrated to you in a direct and dramatic way, and the need to make a change should be just as clear.

It should be evident from this experience that your emotions strongly influence your way of being, and certainly your body. We have only magnified, for purposes of observation, effects which are continuous in your life. We could also have worked with negative emotions. Then you would have a good idea of what you do to yourself when you are chronically angry, fearful, depressed, or filled with self-hatred. Then you would understand very clearly how emotional and mental states can create chronic muscular tensions that displace the skeleton, cause the blood vessels to harden, and even lead the cells to revolt and the body literally to destroy itself. You should understand better that your emotions affect your experience of others, as well as the way other people experience you.

Lie very comfortably, breathe freely, and be as quiet as you can. Just think of being very still. And now imagine and try to feel that there is a membrane separating the two halves of your body. You are going to poke some holes in that membrane. You are going to let the good feelings from the right side move over into the left side. The right side will continue to feel good, but those feelings will fill the left side as well. Move the right side a little, and be conscious once again of the joyousness and the delight.

The membrane is getting very porous now and the holes in it are getting larger. The good feelings are beginning to flow from right to left and, if you pay attention, you may note that the left foot is already catching the happiness. Good warm feelings are suffusing the left foot and ankle, and they can move through the body much faster this time because the right side has already been charged with those feelings and it is only necessary to share them with your left side.

The good feelings and the joyousness are flowing, first of all into the left foot. And now the left hand is catching the delight and is beginning to feel lighter. Move it a little as it begins to feel that way.

Now the left calf is catching the lightness and is being suffused with good feelings. Your left forearm up to the elbow is also receiving the lightness and the joy. There is nothing that you have to do—the good feelings have a momentum of their own. The lightness and joyousness are now moving on up through the left thigh to the hip. The left upper arm and shoulder are becoming light and happy. Move the arm, so that your awareness will increase. The left buttock is becoming a very happy buttock, receiving joy, warmth, and good feelings. Move it as you begin to feel it. More good feelings are moving all through your pelvis on the left and up through your abdomen. Move those parts too and experience them.

Warmth, good feelings, happy emotions moving up through your chest on the left side and on up into your neck. Feel those good feelings and, as you experience them, move and they will become stronger. Move as much of your body as now feels good and happy.

Now the left side of your face is suffused with joy and those good feelings are flowing even more. Move your whole body now and just allow it to sense the warmth and the lightness, the joyousness, the pleasure. See whether the left and the right sides now feel much more alike.

Lie quietly now and observe the way your body feels. Scan your body and note your emotional state. Compare your feelings with those you noted at the beginning of this exercise.

Your nervous system has probably learned a great deal from this experience. You have worked directly on your nervous system with emotional input, and provided yourself with a clear demonstration of the ways in which your emotions affect your body and the ways that you can use emotions to change it. Move around a little more and let your consciousness savor the experience, let your nervous system learn from it, and resolve to remember what you have learned and apply it for your benefit in the future.

Consider that there are almost infinite ways in which you can modify this exercise. You can work with any memories you like, and you can charge your body with any feelings or sensations you care to experience. With practice, you can greatly intensify the experience. Again, in everyday life you do something much like this, but for the most part unconsciously or with barely minimal awareness. If you consciously and deliberately charge your body with good feelings and positive emotions, then your hedonistic nervous system should come to prefer those feelings and emotions, so that they will become your normal and habitual way of being.

Further Applications of a Method

THE TEACHING METHOD we have presented in this book, making use of what we have called the "seduction of consciousness by novelty," has a very wide range of applications. The next exercise will teach you how to focus your complete attention on an object for much longer than you could otherwise, at least without prolonged and arduous training in special techniques of concentration and meditation. In fact, the effects you will observe will be similar to those of meditation as most people practice it. You will probably experience an overall sense of relaxation and, as you contemplate the object from many different perspectives, it will become almost numinous and alive, and somehow seem more real than the other objects around it.

The creation of most of the exercises in this book required a high degree of bodily awareness and a quite detailed knowledge of body mechanics. In the same way, you will be able to invent new exercises of your own only after you have learned to use your body as a laboratory for experimental work. With a little ingenuity, though, anyone should be able to come up with new applications of this basic method, such as the exercise you are about to try. Further applications can be of great help to us in many kinds of problem-solving and in reawakening memories, and to the psychotherapist in understanding a patient's relationships to others, especially to key figures in his life, more quickly than would ordinarily be possible.

The exercise calls for several objects: a large book, a small table, and a carpet for the table to stand on. (If you do not have one or more of these objects, then it should be a simple matter to make the necessary substitutions or omissions.)

Sit in a position that is comfortable. You should have before you, a few feet away, a large book resting on a small table; the table should be standing on a carpet of some kind. You are going to learn to keep your attention on these objects, especially the book, for about forty-five minutes, without making much of an effort. We will help you to concentrate unwaveringly; the mind will not drift off as you think about other things. We will help you to keep from being preoccupied with sensations that have nothing to do with the object. We will work together with you to maintain the relationship between you (the subject) and the object, letting as little as possible—and finally nothing that is extraneous—intrude into the relationship.

Now look at the book very carefully and begin to observe what it is that you perceive. You notice that the book is resting on its side on top of a table which, in turn, is standing on a carpet.

You notice not only the color of the table and the carpet, but the colors of the book, the printing on the binding or the jacket of the book, the edges of the paper, the flat surface of the cover of the book.

Your perception of colors is determined in part, of course, by the amount of light in the room and the direction from which the light is coming. It should be easy to imagine other lighting—a bright light over the book, or a spotlight shining on the spine of the book, or the book by candlelight, or the book in a very dimly lighted room.

As you look at it, note the relationship of the book to the floor, and that the book has a relation to the ceiling, a relation to the wall to your left, a relation to the wall to the right. That book occupies a position in space defined by its relations to what is above it, below it, and on all sides of it. It has a special relationship to you, to the table, and to any object you choose to relate it to.

Think about the thickness of the book. One thing that determines the book's thickness, of course, is the number of pages it has. But the thickness of the individual pages is important, and the thickness of the binding.

Try to imagine the pages: what it is like to open the book and hold just the binding, how thick it feels, how it feels in general, and then what it feels like to hold a page between your fingers, a few pages, and then many.

If you opened the book you would probably find that the inside of the binding is blank and that the first page is also blank, not on just one side, but on both. Then the page after that may have just the title, and then there is a page with the title, the name of the author, the publisher, and other information about the book.

Think about and imagine reading the book. As you look at page after page after page, the book will yield more and more information, or, if it is a novel, a tale will unfold. And it will reveal more and more of its contents as you go deeper and deeper into it.

The book has an author, or authors, and it has had an editor, or editors, a publisher, printers, someone who bound the book, someone who delivered it to the bookstore, and someone who sold it. Think about some of those processes involved—writing, editing, publishing, bookbinding, distributing, and selling. But think about them in relation to the book you are observing.

The book has come out of the experience of the author, or authors. What kind of experience was required? How much is a product of imagination, and what kind of imagination? There is research, there is the physical task of writing, sitting long hours at the typewriter, and then finding a publisher who will take the manuscript. Then waiting for the finished book to arrive and, when finally it comes, the author holding the book in his hands, or hers, looking through it, and the feelings about having the book, and wondering about how the book is going to be received.

Think in more detail about the offices of the publisher where the book was edited, and all the other manuscripts there in various stages of becoming printed books. Think of the printer as he sets the type, and the proofreader reading the proofs. Keep looking at the book on the table, and imagine it, or another copy of the same book, arriving at the bookstore, someone taking it out of its box, and someone deciding how it will be displayed.

Think about this book on a shelf or a table in the bookstore, waiting to be purchased, to be taken home, to be read, and to communicate the knowledge it contains; other copies of the book read by many people, many minds taking from it and interpreting it according to their own experience and learning.

Think of the book as a book that many people have opened, leafed through, read, and found valuable or have found entertaining or dull.

Think of the book, most of the time reposing on a shelf, but now sitting there on that little table right before you; and of your own ways of relating to that book, what meaning it has for you.

The book could have been somewhat different. It could have been thicker—if the author had written more pages, or if the publisher had chosen thicker paper. There are many colors the book might have been other than the color it is. Think of it as being different colors. Think of it as being thicker, and as being thinner.

Think of what it would feel like to touch it right now with the palm of your hand. What it would feel like depends, of course, on where you touch it. Touching it with the back of your hand would be a different experience, as would resting your cheek on it, or touching it with your nose or your ear or your lips or your tongue or with just your fingernails.

You could be closer to the book, sitting up very close to it where you could touch it, or just out of reach, or where you are now. Try to imagine your perception of the book as depending upon how far away from it you are.

You could stand up and look down at the book. Think about walking around it, looking at the bottom edge of the pages, and at the top edge. Continue to walk around it and look at the binding, and the opposite edge of the book, and just keep circling around it in your imagination. You could see it from higher up, looking down, or you could lie on the floor and look up at it.

Now for a minute or so try to see the book just as clearly as you possibly can from the perspective not of any imaginary relationships but from precisely where you are. See every bit of the book's surface that you can see—the colors, the textures, the immediate area around the book. Try to look at that book and see everything that there is to see about it, and see it as clearly and unwaveringly as possible, paying attention to nothing else at all.

Now, as you continue looking at the book, try to observe whether the color of the binding on the top remains constant or whether it seems to change as you continue to stare at it. Is the lighting constant? Does the book stay flat or seem to bulge? Do the lines along the edges of the book stay flat, or do they seem to curve a little? On the edge of the book, is something changing there? Do you see the book as exactly the same at all times, or as you look at it fixedly does anything change?

Now, as you look at the book, try to imagine that you are in a place where time passes very quickly, a great deal of time passes very, very quickly, and you are very conscious of the passage of time as you look at the book.

Look at the book and imagine yourself in a place where time passes very, very slowly. You have all of the time you could want. Time passes very, very slowly.

Now imagine youself in a place out of time, a timeless space where you and the book are unchanging, because where there is no time, there is no change. You have always been the same and will always be the same.

And think of the book as not only unchanging but as the prototype or archetype of books, as The Book. It represents all books. In a sense everything that is meant by "book" or was ever understood by "book," every perception of "book" is contained in that one book there before you. Think about the bookness of that object and let it speak for all books.

While you are looking, think about the relationship

between human beings and books, what the book means to us, and has meant, what the invention of printing meant, the explosion of knowledge, the possibility of universal education, the transmission of knowledge among people, the enormous transformation of man and of society that the book made possible.

There was a time when a man looking at the book would see an absolutely magical and sacred thing, an object of power that was also seen as a gift from God: It was so powerful that he would feel reverence and awe in its presence. All human knowledge now could be placed between the covers of books, those books put into libraries, and those libraries would then contain the worthwhile knowledge of the ages, the products of all the great minds, the great ideas and great discoveries and inventions, everything could be preserved in that way. A thought like that simply staggered the minds of men. Look at the book in front of you and try to get even a faint sense of how someone in the past might have felt about it. Men looked at books where no books had been before and realized the power that was there between those covers, and the implications for humanity.

Now just look at the book as a material object for your senses to deal with, and try to imagine with great clarity what it feels like to open the book and leaf through its pages: the sounds the pages make. Try to remember the smell of the book, what some of its pages look like, how it feels to look at a page, to read, and feel the movement of the eyes reading a page, how you hold the book, how you sit holding the book in front of you.

Imagine that the book is very warm. It could have been left in the sun; it would then be very warm to the touch. You could rest your head on it and use it for a pillow. It could be very warm. It could burn. It could be smouldering, or scorched.

It could also be rained on, or be immersed in water. If it were wet and cold, it could freeze. The book could be encased in ice. Imagine the book frozen, what it would be like. First it would be wet and later, when it dried, its pages would crumple.

Now look at it again, just as it is. Once again try to see it clearly. Fix your attention on it. See whether the book is now more stable than it was earlier. The light does not keep changing so much. The outlines of the book are steadier. It is fixed, firmly defined by all its relationships to the things around it, and becoming more commonplace, becoming just another book.

Then continue to look at it and see if it is not, in fact, a special book. The book exists for you now in a special way. Pay close attention and think of all the ways you have experienced the book, all the perspectives you have had on it. Take a couple of minutes to focus intensely on the book and try to think of the perspectives on that book that you've gone over since the exercise began—philosophical, historical, artistic, scholarly, spatial, temporal, sensory, all those different perspectives in relation to that book. For the next couple of minutes review them while looking at the book with the greatest intensity you can summon.

Now get up slowly and walk around a little, whenever you are ready to do it. Take a look around the room, and then sit back down.

Look at the book and look around at other objects in the room. See whether you tend to return to that book, and whether the book now has a quality that the other objects do not have, whether it has an individuality and a greater fullness of being than the other objects in the room, as if somehow your attention had charged it and given it a special meaning for you which demands that you perceive it in a special way. Many people will find that when they have contemplated and considered and concentrated on an object as you have done for a period of time, then for a little while it becomes almost numinous and seems somehow more real than the objects around it. It has an *essential* quality. A famous Van Gogh painting of a chair captures that kind of perception very well—wherein one object assumes a special importance and stands out from all the rest as though it were the essential or ideal object.

It would be almost impossible by any other means than the one that we just demonstrated to keep your attention focused as intently as it was on that book for the same length of time. Try to think of any other way you might do it and you will recognize how difficult it is. This way the senses, at least, can learn to focus themselves with a minimum of effort and discomfort. The body learns to tolerate prolonged immobility and to a degree the mind also learns to focus itself. Most important, the object is at last perceived without associations and the other usual distractions—it is seen "purely," and thus is differentiated from other objects, which are seen in the ordinary way. That is the goal of the lesson and, as we remarked at the beginning of this chapter, the same method can be applied to problems and memories, so that they too can be seen "purely."

The method will serve you if you cooperate with it. If, even with this approach, your mind still wanders or your body distracts you, then it will be necessary to practice if you wish to work successfully with this method.

Movement—Music—Meditation

LIKE MEDITATION, all of the psychophysical exercises require that you focus your attention. It is essential not to allow your mind to stray away from the performance and uninterrupted experience of the exercises. We have emphasized novelty and variety in designing the exercises, but you should still make a special effort to keep your attention focused and to be particularly aware of the sensations produced by the exercises. Then you will be able to re-create the experience not just visually but through all the senses, tactile and kinesthetic especially.

You should try to practice the exercises by imagining that you are experiencing them through all your senses. You may eventually be able to construct an

imaginary body which can be sensed as entirely separate from the physical body. Your sensations of this
imaginary body's activities will help to improve the actual functioning of the physical body; if you are immobilized by some injury, the imaginary body can be
used to exercise the physical body and facilitate its re-
covery. The doctrine of "subtle bodies," common to all
ancient psychophysical traditions, affirms the mind's
potential to create and use such an imaginary body for
self-healing and improving athletic, artistic, and many
other types of performance.

You might begin to imagine this subtle body by alternately performing various actions with the physical
body and then imagining the same actions. For example, fully extend your left arm; carefully note the
sensations associated with raising your arm and holding it out to the side. Slowly bring your arm down to
your side and note the sensations, how your side feels
to your arm and hand, how your arm and hand feel to
your side. Imagine that you extend your arm again,
how it feels to raise the arm and to extend it. Actually
extend your arm, then imagine that you are bringing it
down to your side; imagine the contact of your arm
and hand with your body. Imagine how your hand and
arm and body sense one another.

If you repeat this exercise often enough and try to
experience your imaginary movements as vividly as
possible, you should not be able to distinguish the actual from the imaginary parts of the exercise with your
eyes closed. The nervous system will be incapable of
distinguishing subjective and objective reality. The

same exercise can be repeated until many different parts of the body can be simultaneously moved in the imagination and, finally, a complete imaginary body has come into being. (This is, of course, an advanced psychophysical exercise, which you may not care to attempt.)

You can also benefit by temporarily breaking down the body image, which will relax not only the body but the structure of the ego as well, providing a significant mental and emotional release. This is a very pleasurable exercise which, if included in a series of other exercises, will provide an enjoyable change of pace and help motivate you to carry out the entire exercise program.

The effects are achieved by what we will call Movement–Music–Meditation, by which we mean a great variety of movements taken from the entire program (and including any improvisations you might care to try). All (or almost all) are performed with the body more or less flat on the floor. This partially counteracts the force of gravity, so that you will be able to notice changes in the body image more readily than if the body remained upright (as in the prolonged dances performed in many cultures to achieve similar results).

Like most of the other exercises, this one should be performed for at least forty-five minutes, although sessions should sometimes be extended to ninety minutes, two hours, or even longer. You will soon find out, however, that this can be a thoroughly pleasurable experience, and you will have little difficulty in occasionally extending these sessions.

Selecting the right music is very important, of course. Try to choose music that seems very physical to you, that will be conducive to continuous sensuous movement. There are various ethnic recordings available of folk music, chants, trance music, and so on, which are intended specifically to induce altered states of consciousness. You might explore the music of Polynesia and Bali, Sufi chanting, and especially some of the recorded Indian sitar music. We have found that some of the truly hypnotic recorded performances by Ravi Shankar (without vocal) have been very helpful to our research subjects. (If possible, transfer your records to reel-to-reel tape at 1⅞ speed, so that a single tape can play for two or three hours without interruption.)

A good way to begin might be to remember a number of movements from previous exercises and run through a series of them, fitting the movements to the music so that the exercise will begin to seem more like a dance. Make the exercise as sensuous and as pleasurable as possible; involve your entire body in the experience of physical, mental, and emotional pleasure. Lose yourself in the music and the physical sensations of movement; your consciousness will gradually be captivated; after that, the experience of this pleasure can become your entire reality. (This total immersion will be easier to sustain if there are no interruptions to change the recording or otherwise, and if, of course, your physical position on the floor is completely comfortable.)

After a while, you will sense that the body image is

changing, that movement is becoming lighter and easier. Eventually, your body will feel insubstantial and flowing. Often, beautiful organic imagery will accompany this change, and sometimes very primitive feelings of animal vitality—as if you were breaking through layers of inhibition and obstruction to reach the feelings beneath.

Then you may feel that your body is made of tongues of fire or particles of energy moving in a sinuous, serpentine flow. Feelings of fatigue and effort vanish completely, ordinary restrictions on your body are no longer operating. This seems actually to be true. For example, at this point you will be able to stand up from your reclining position on the floor and then lie down again many times without any apparent increase in heartbeat or respiration.

You should work up to these prolonged experiences somewhat gradually and note your reactions. The great majority of people who enjoy normal health will soon be able to extend these sessions to two hours or more. Then you can begin to dissolve the body image and immerse yourself in an extremely enjoyable and refreshing experience, mentally, physically, and emotionally. And then you will be ready to take another step into the as yet unsolved and always fascinating mysteries of our being.

Conclusions

PSYCHOPHYSICAL REEDUCATION is a powerful force that could transform society if it were widely applied. The method is of very great therapeutic value, can increase both health and longevity, and can improve human functioning in general by promoting good use and awareness.

Taught to children as a preventative discipline, the method would enable people to avoid those tensions, unconscious and barely conscious actions, and sensory impairments which eventually damage health, produce many mental and emotional problems, and block actualization of thinking, feeling, sensing, and movement potentials. In the case of older children and adults, the method can prevent further damage from occurring while undoing much of the harm that already has been done.

Especially striking results can be obtained with the elderly. Those who can be motivated to do the work required will discover that many of the so-called symptoms of old age are readily reversible, so that not only can pain and stiffness be relieved and movement very greatly improved, but many apparent symptoms of senility also will be greatly reduced or done away with altogether. These physical and mental improvements will enhance self-esteem and self-confidence and reawaken the interest in and zest for life.

Therapeutically, reeducation has achieved astonishing successes in the areas of rheumatic disorders, neurological disorders, spinal disorders, breathing disorders, stress diseases, rehabilitation, pain relief, psychosomatic and mental disorders, and pre- and postnatal care.

The psychotherapist who has gained sufficient awareness and ability to use psychophysical techniques will find himself better able to diagnose as well as to treat his patients' problems. He will understand much better, and see more clearly, the bodily components of emotional and mental disorders. Then he will be able to work with the whole person, eliminating, for example, the patient's patterns of muscular tensions which are as much a part of his neurosis as are his anxiety, phobia, depression, and whatever other problems constitute his syndrome. And the patient, having gained sufficient awareness and ability to sense and eliminate his tensions, will not allow them to reaccumulate and thus bring back the associated mental symptoms, as all too often occurs.

Psychophysical methods can be used therapeutically or for rehabilitation, but they also can improve performance of athletes and dancers and others who have spent years attempting to bring themselves to a peak of fitness, coordination, agility, strength, sensitivity, or whatever else may be required for their particular objectives. What the exercises demonstrate is that further improvement is always possible and within reach.

In our experience, the regular and long-term practice of exercises such as those contained in this book will yield all of the effects we have described, and more. Eventually, as with the practice of yoga and other psychophysical disciplines, the neural reeducation will bring about changes not produced by ordinary types of exercise. More will be sensed, and the thinking processes will become more lucid and, for some, more logical. The capacity to specifically alter states of consciousness is also within reach, including what for this method is the most desirable state—a degree of wakefulness and awareness which frees the person from coercion either from within or from without. Such freedom will not come easily or quickly, and for all but a few it will occur only intermittently. Even so, this method brings inspiring and beneficial glimpses of that wakefulness and autonomy which are man's potential and toward which humanity would seem to be evolving.

Selected Bibliography

ALEXANDER, F. M. *Man's Supreme Inheritance.* London: Chaterston, 1946.

———. *The Use of the Self.* London: Re-Educational Publications, 1955.

———. *The Resurrection of the Body.* New York: Delta Books, 1969.

BARLOW, WILFRED. *The Alexander Principle.* London: Arrow Books, 1975.

———. *The Alexander Technique.* New York: Alfred A. Knopf, 1973.

BERTHERAT, THÉRÈSE, and BERNSTEIN, CAROL. *The Body Has Its Reasons: Anti-Exercises and Self-Awareness.* New York: Pantheon Books, 1977.

ECCLES, JOHN C. *Facing Reality: Philosophical Adventures by a Brain Scientist.* New York: Springer-Verlag, 1970.

FELDENKRAIS, MOSHE. *Awareness Through Movement: Health Exercises for Personal Growth.* New York: Harper & Row, 1972.

————. *Body and Mature Behavior: A Study of Anxiety, Sex, Gravitation & Learning.* New York: International Universities Press, 1970.

————. *The Case of Nora.* New York: Harper & Row, 1977.

HALEY, JAY, ed. *Advanced Techniques of Hypnosis and Therapy: Selected Papers of Milton H. Erickson, M.D.* New York: Grune & Stratton, 1967.

HEATH, R., ed. *The Role of Pleasure in Behavior.* New York: Harper & Row, 1964.

IYENGAR, B. K. *Light on Yoga.* New York: Schocken Books, 1972.

JACOBSON, EDMUND. *Progressive Relaxation.* Chicago: The University of Chicago Press, 1938.

JONES, FRANK P. *Body Awareness in Action: A Study of the Alexander Technique.* New York: Schocken Books, 1976.

LURIA, A. R. *The Mind of a Mnemonist: A Little Book About a Vast Memory.* Translated by Lynn Solotaroff. New York: Basic Books, 1968.

MASTERS, ROBERT, and HOUSTON, JEAN. *Mind Games: The Guide to Inner Space.* New York: Delta Books, 1973.

NEEDLEMAN, JACOB. *A Sense of the Cosmos.* New York: Doubleday, 1975.

PENFIELD, WILDER. *The Mystery of the Mind: A Critical Study of Consciousness and the Human Brain.* Princeton: Princeton University Press, 1975.

PRIBRAM, KARL H. *Languages of the Brain: Experimental Paradoxes and Principles in Neuropsychology.* New Jersey: Prentice Hall, 1971.

SCHILDER, PAUL. *The Image & Appearance of the Human Body.* New York: Science Editions, 1964.

————. *Mind: Perception and Thought in Their Constructive Aspects.* New York: Columbia University Press, 1942.

SHELTON, HERBERT M. *Exercise!* Chicago: Natural Hygiene Press, 1971.

SHERRINGTON, CHARLES S. *Man on His Nature.* Cambridge: Cambridge University Press, 1951.

SPERANSKY, A. *A Basis for the Theory of Medicine.* New York: International Publishers, undated.

SWEIGARD, LULU E. *Human Movement Potential: Its Ideokinetic Facilitation.* New York: Dodd, Mead & Company, 1974.

TINBERGEN, N. "Ethology and Stress Diseases." *Science,* Vol. 185, No. 4145 (July 5, 1974), pp. 20–27.

TODD, MABEL E. *The Thinking Body: A Study of Balancing Forces of Dynamic Man.* New York: Dance Horizons, 1975.

VAN DURCKHEIM, KARLFRIED GRAF, *Daily Life as Spiritual Exercise.* New York: Harper & Row, 1972.

————. *Hara: The Vital Centre of Man.* New York: Fernhill House, 1970.

YOUNG, J. Z. *The Memory System of the Brain.* Berkeley: University of California Press, 1966.

Audio tapes of psychophysical exercises are available. Interested persons should contact Drs. Robert Masters and Jean Houston, P.O. Box 600, Pomona, N.Y. 10970.